T0279385

BLACK COWBOYS
AND
EARLY CATTLE DRIVES

BLACK COWBOYS
AND
EARLY CATTLE DRIVES

ON THE TRAILS FROM
TEXAS TO MONTANA

NANCY WILLIAMS

THE
History
PRESS

Published by The History Press
Charleston, SC
www.historypress.com

Copyright © 2023 by Nancy K. Williams
All rights reserved

First published 2023

Manufactured in the United States

ISBN 9781467153645

Library of Congress Control Number: 2022951607

Notice: The information in this book is true and complete to the best of our knowledge. It is offered without guarantee on the part of the author or The History Press. The author and The History Press disclaim all liability in connection with the use of this book.

All rights reserved. No part of this book may be reproduced or transmitted in any form whatsoever without prior written permission from the publisher except in the case of brief quotations embodied in critical articles and reviews.

For Tom. Thanks for your patience and perseverance.

THE OLD COWBOY

I rode a line on the open range
When cow-punchin' wasn't slow.
I've turned the longhorn cow one way,
And the other the buffalo.
I went up the trail in the eighties—
Oh, the hardships I have stood
I've drank the water from cow tracks, Boys,
When you bet it tasted good.
I've stood guard many a night
In the face of a driving storm
And sang to them a doleful song
When they rattled their hocks and horns.
I've been in many a stampede, too:
I've heard the rumbling noise
And the light we had to turn them by
Was the lightning on their horns.
They're building towns and railroads now
Where we used to bed our cows;
And the man with the mule, the plow, and the hoe
Is digging up our old bed grounds.
The old cowboy has watched the change
Has seen the good times come and go—
But the old cowboy will soon be gone,
Just like the buffalo.

CONTENTS

ACKNOWLEDGEMENTS

A big thank-you to Tom Williams for locating, editing, and compiling the historic photos published in this book. The photographs of cowboys, trail drives, and work on the ranch are greatly appreciated and have added a lot of interesting content.

Thanks to the many regional and local historical associations that have answered my questions and provided information about Black cowboys, pioneers, and ranchers. Thank you for sharing your photograph collections and allowing their use.

The Black American West Museum of Denver has an impressive collection of memorabilia, artifacts, exhibits, and displays about Black cowboys, homesteaders, and pioneers in the nineteenth-century West. The museum is in Denver in the former home of Colorado's first Black woman doctor, Dr. Justina Ford.

The Goodnight Barn west of Pueblo was built by the famed cattleman in 1869. He purchased a large piece of rolling land west of Pueblo, built a ranch house and barn, and moved his cattle business from Texas to Colorado. More than a century later, the Goodnight Barn is the only structure remaining of this once flourishing ranch. It is one of the oldest surviving buildings in Colorado, and in 2020, it was purchased by Colorado Preservation Inc., a nonprofit organization, and the City of Pueblo. It has been restored with $1 million raised by the Goodnight Barn Preservation Committee and other organizations.

Historically, the offensive "n-word" was often used in conjunction with a Black man's first name. It has been omitted in this book, and only the first names of Black cowboys are used with their surnames when they were available.

INTRODUCTION

Longhorn cattle were brought to America in the 1500s by Cortez and early Spanish explorers. The cattle thrived, and within twenty-five years, thousands were running wild in Mexico. Over the next two centuries, Franciscan priests and Spanish settlers moved north from Mexico and crossed the Rio Grande, taking their cattle and horses to Texas. The priests were intent on converting the local Indians to Christianity and built Mission San Antonio de Valero, the Alamo, in 1718. A small village developed near the mission where settlers farmed and raised cattle, sheep, goats, and horses. Some of the Spanish cattle escaped, roved about, and hid in the brush. They grew larger and heavy-boned and were wily, unpleasant beasts with fiery tempers and dangerous, long horns that were offensive weapons. By 1821, when the first colonists came, wild longhorns had overrun Texas.

Most colonists were from the southern United States, and they settled along the East Texas coast, bringing slaves to work in the fields and care for their cattle and horses. Mexico did not favor slavery and threatened to abolish it in Texas, but settlers believed that slaves were needed to raise cotton, which was vital for economic growth. There were about five thousand slaves in Texas, about 13 percent of the population. The dispute over slavery was the main reason Texans revolted against Mexico in 1835–36.

After Texas became an independent republic, with Sam Houston as its first elected president, its constitution and congress protected slavery and the slave trade. The constitution forbade the emancipation of slaves by individuals without congressional approval. If an owner freed his slaves, they had to leave Texas because their presence could undermine the practice of slavery.

Slaves in Texas were personal property and could be bought and sold, mortgaged, and hired out. They had no property rights, no legal rights of marriage and family, and no legally prescribed way to gain their freedom. Some slaves were skilled craftsmen, while others were house servants; the majority were field hands or worked with livestock. Many settlers with small farms owned ten or fewer slaves, but like all slave owners, they believed that theirs were essential. Slavery expanded during the decade Texas was a republic, and by 1846, when it was annexed to the United States, at least thirty thousand Black people were enslaved there. By 1850, there were forty-eight thousand slaves in Texas, and as slavery expanded, the number of longhorns also grew rapidly.

Wild longhorns adapted to their environment, whether it was in the thorny brush country, the coastal plains, the plateaus, or the rolling Texas Hill Country. They roamed in small groups during the night and stayed hidden during the day. They were relatively disease resistant and able to survive in a harsh environment, and the cows produced and raised a calf every year. Cows identified their calves by smell rather than sight and, if separated, could usually find them again.

These wild, slab-sided, ornery longhorns weighed between 1,000 and 1,500 pounds and had long tails that often dragged on the ground. Just like horses, longhorns came in all colors, and they didn't look alike. They were hardy and could tolerate heat, blizzards, drought, swarms of fierce insects, and poor forage. They could walk miles to water on their boney, sturdy legs and hard hooves. They were sneaky, cunning, and vicious when irritated, and they didn't hesitate to use their fearsome, sharp, pointed horns. By 1840, these wild cattle had become a recognizable breed, the Texas longhorn.

Settlers who moved into central and northwest Texas decided to become cattlemen when they saw the vast numbers of roaming wild longhorns and the abundant grass and lush pastureland. It wasn't too difficult to become a cowman: a fellow only needed a rope, a branding iron, and the nerve to use them to capture the unbranded longhorns. The wild brutes hid in thickets and brushy river bottoms, and since most settlers didn't have their land fenced, the cattle were free to roam about. Longhorns were built for speed with their long legs, and it took a fast horse to outrun them. They could walk farther and go longer without water than domesticated cattle. When angered or wounded,

Longhorn cattle on the George Ranch Historical Park, a twenty-thousand-acre working ranch in Fort Bend County, Texas, featuring historic homes, costumed interpreters, and livestock. *Carol Highsmith, Library of Congress.*

they were vicious and would fight any living thing. Their lethal horns had a spread of four to eight feet, making them formidable foes.

Most of the Texas settlers owned 5 to 10 slaves, who helped them establish a new life: building a cabin, putting up a barn, and erecting corrals to contain livestock. By 1850, there were about 58,000 slaves in Texas, with each worth about $400. By 1860, their value had increased to about $800, and as slavery expanded in Texas, prices became inflated even more. A male field hand eighteen to thirty years old cost $1,200, while a skilled slave, like a blacksmith, was valued at more than $2,000. Slave owners were taxed for their human property at the same rate they paid for cattle or land, and antebellum tax records show that slaves were occasionally traded for cattle. Ambitious would-be cattlemen, impressed with the possibilities of raising cattle in Texas, even sold a few of their slaves to buy cows and calves to start their ranching enterprises. Texas State Historical Association records show that by 1860 there were 182,566 slaves in Texas, making them 30.2 percent of the entire population.

Mexican cowboys called *vaqueros* taught slaves how to lasso steers and use a branding iron and the rudiments of handling longhorns. There were more Black ranch hands in East Texas and fewer in arid, sparsely settled West

Black cowboy with his horse. *Denver Public Library Western History Collection, [X-21563].*

Texas or the bleak southern region, which was choked by dense thickets of thorny chaparral and mesquite. Prickly pear cactus grew everywhere, and while the plants provided vital moisture to wild longhorns, the nasty thorns got stuck in every part of a cowboy's anatomy. Longhorns had to be driven out of the brush or roped and dragged from their hiding places, and the furious animals often charged a horse or a man on foot.

Before the Civil War, the word *cowboy* itself was racially specific and demeaning. In Texas, where slaves were as likely to be working in the cotton field as the corral with horses and cattle, Black men were often called "boy." This was a disrespectful term and when paired with "cow" referred to a slave handling livestock. A white man working on a ranch in the same capacity was a "ranch hand." White men who worked with cattle called themselves "drovers, cattlemen, stockmen, or traders." Ironically, over time, the word *cowboy* came to mean any man, regardless of color, who did much of his job herding and tending cattle on horseback. As the years passed, cowboys were admired as adventurous, bold, brave, daring, and independent men on horseback, capable of heroic deeds.

Samuel Maverick came to Texas around 1835 to acquire land and accepted a herd of four hundred longhorns as payment of a debt. Settlers in southern Texas, who were starting to raise cattle, met to describe their unique brands and earmarks. Maverick refused to brand his cattle or mark their ears and declared that all unmarked cattle belonged to him. Surprisingly, the others agreed, and soon they were referring to any unbranded animal as "one of Maverick's." His cattle were neglected and roamed unchecked over a wide area. Settlers trying to accumulate their own herds started rounding up these unclaimed cattle as "mavericks" and branding them in a common practice soon known as "mavericking." These maverick longhorns became the foundation of the new herds of many Texas cattlemen.

Despite the Emancipation Proclamation of September 22, 1862, slaves in Texas remained in bondage. More than two and a half years passed between Lincoln's proclamation and the formal end of slavery in Texas. Freedom finally came on June 19, 1865, Juneteenth, when Union army general Gordon Granger issued General Order Number 3, announcing the end of slavery in Texas. The order declared that "all slaves are free" and that the relationship between master and slave would be considered as "that between employer and hired labor." By the end of the Civil War, slaves who had been managing the herds, tracking longhorns, branding calves, and breaking and training mustangs so they could be ridden had become a valuable part the growing Texas cattle industry.

SLAVES BECOME COWBOYS

Confederate veterans returned from the Civil War to find their property overrun with wild longhorns in some areas; in others, their herds were gone, scattered into the brush. Cattlemen, anxious to build longhorn herds, held cow hunts to round up the roaming cattle and drive them into sturdy corrals built in strategic locations. Cowboys from neighboring ranches worked together, spending days in the saddle, battling the brush, mud, dust, snakes, and ferocious mosquitoes.

Cows hid their new calves in the brush, while the shaggy steers crawled through thorny thickets like snakes and were ready to fight. Some of these mavericks had never had a cowboy's lasso around their wrinkled necks, and getting a bunch of these outlaws from the brush to the corral was murderous work. The angry steers were ready to hook anything in their way with their sharp horns.

Occasionally, a steer made a break for it and escaped back into the brush. The weary cowboys chased these renegades down, roped them once again, and sometimes tied the worst to a tree for the night. Hopefully by morning, this stubborn mossy horn would be a bit more cooperative and could be driven into a herd that was being moved to the ranch.

After a few days of cow hunting in one area, the cow camp and chuck wagon were moved to another spot, and the cow hunt began again. After working several weeks, at least one thousand or more cattle would be gathered in the corrals. The animals were herded tightly together to decrease the chance of their knocking down fences and stampeding. At night, the cattle were guarded by shifts of mounted cowboys, who rode around the enclosure singing to calm them.

The cattle boom that began after the Civil War provided employment for many emancipated Black men who had worked cattle and broken horses for their former owners. Ranchers hired these skilled Black cowboys as paid cowhands to work alongside white cowboys. "Right after the Civil War, being a cowboy was one of the few jobs open to men of color who didn't want to serve as elevator operators, delivery boys, or similar occupations," said William Katz, an expert on African American history. When ranchers began selling cattle to eastern markets, more cowboys were needed to drive large herds to railroad shipping points in Colorado, Kansas, and Missouri.

During the more than two decades of great cattle drives, there was an astronomical demand for cowboys. It's estimated that at least 25 percent of the cattle industry's workforce was Black and that one out of every four cowboys on the trail was Black. About 12 percent were Mexican. Ranch records and those of cattle drives often didn't include a cowboy's ethnicity, but many listed Black cowboys simply as Jim or Ed. Black cowboys were wranglers, cowhands, bronc busters, and horse trainers. The Black cowboys were good workers and got along well with others. Older, experienced Black cowhands were often more willing to show the ropes to younger white men than other white cowboys.

Like longhorns, there were plenty of wild mustangs running free, and ranchers rounded them up to use herding cattle. Breaking and training them was a task that often went to the Black cowboys. Some mustangs had to start their day with a few bucks before they'd settle down, while others were determined to go through their entire repertoire before they were fit to ride. Most cowboys didn't want to ride a pony that was "inclined to jump out of his skin or throw the hair off his back." It was often the Black cowboy's job to take the starch out of these horses. Once he was in the saddle, the show began—a rodeo every day! While the other cowboys were eating breakfast in the kitchen or around the campfire, the Black man was greeting the rising sun from the back of a stubbornly twisting, "sun-fishing" mustang. The horse jumped high, turning in the air, swapping ends with his head where his tail once was, and then hitting the ground with all fours. Once that horse settled down, there was usually another one waiting, intent on sending anyone who climbed on his back skyward. This daily ordeal was called "topping off," and the task often fell to a Black cowboy who was good at riding broncs. An article in the February 1916 issue of *Cattleman Magazine* said, "It was not unusual for one young Negro to 'top' a half-dozen pitching horses before

A Black cowboy sits on his saddled horse in Pocatello, Idaho, in 1903. *Smithsonian.*

breakfast." Cowboys dreaded these morning hijinks and appreciated the Black cowboys who rode the ornery mustangs for them. "Old Ad" (Addison Jones), praised as "the most noted Negro cowboy that ever topped off a horse," never hesitated to climb into the saddle for a cowboy reluctant to shake up his breakfast on an ornery bronc.

Most ranches had one or two outlaw horses that were "as bad as any ever wore hair," but they could be straightened out by cowboys like Old Ad, Jim Kelly, or Ned Huddleston, better known as Isom Dart. Born enslaved in 1849, Dart held a variety of jobs—some lawful, some not. He was a successful horse thief, but he decided to try raising cattle honestly in Brown's Hole, a remote area along the Colorado-Wyoming border favored by outlaws. When Ned needed money, he trapped and broke wild mustangs, and he was very successful.

George Fletcher bronc busting at Pendleton Round-Up Rodeo, Oregon, in 1911. *W.S. Bowman, National Cowboy & Western Heritage Museum.*

Unfortunately, Ned deviated from the straight and narrow and joined a gang of horse thieves. This turned out badly when every member of the gang was killed except Ned, who hightailed it back to Oklahoma. After several years there, he returned to Brown's Hole and began stocking his small ranch with "borrowed" cattle. He was arrested several times for rustling but was always acquitted. Then a Wyoming sheriff nabbed him and headed north, intending to try him for rustling far from a friendly Colorado jury. On the way, the buckboard in which they were riding crashed off a cliff, and the sheriff was injured. Ned took him to town, where he was hospitalized. Then Ned turned himself in to a deputy. At his Wyoming trial, likable Ned was acquitted once again because the jury reasoned that since he had rescued their sheriff, he certainly was not a menace to society.

Ned returned to Brown's Hole, but Wyoming cattlemen were hiring "regulators," who were really hired killers, to rid their range of rustlers. Unfortunately, Ned was on their list, and on October 3, 1900, when he walked out of his cabin to greet the rising sun, he was shot in the back by Tom Horn. His funeral was attended by hundreds, who eulogized Ned

Ned Huddleston, aka "Isom Dart." Brown's Hole, Colorado. *Public domain.*

Huddleston, aka Isom Dart, and praised his skill at taming wild horses. Despite his chronic difficulty with the concepts of "what's mine" and "what's thine," they mourned "a good man who was always helpful."

"I used to rather ketch up a wild horse and break 'em, than to eat breakfast," reminisced William Green, who was twelve years old when he arrived at the ranch where his new master raised and trained wild horses. I was a "buckerman," he said. "By the time I was 12, I could break horses alongside the best of 'em!" William was one of many Black cowboys interviewed about their lives in Texas during the nineteenth and early twentieth centuries. Their stories were among more than 2,300 collected in the 1930s as part of the Federal Writers' Project of the Works Progress Administration and published in the *Slave Narratives*.

There are narratives from many slaves as young as six years old, who were cook's helpers and wranglers on cattle drives. Henry Lewis was owned by Bob Cole, and when he was six years old, he decided that "I's big enuf to start ridin' horses. I's too li'l to git on de hoss and dey lift me up and dey have de real saddle for me. I couldn't git up but I sho' could stay up when I git dere, I's jes' like a hoss fly." Lewis remembered branding longhorns and, like the others, said he had plenty of beef and bacon to eat.

Monroe Brackens came to Texas with his sisters and parents, slaves of Master George Reedes. When he was six years old, he had "some shoes to keep the thorns out of my feet and rawhide leggings." As a young cowhand on the Adams ranch on the Hondo River, he said, "Master came out and told us we were as free as he was. Told us we could stay and work or we could go on if we wanted to." Brackens broke mustangs and said, "We'd ketch 'em up, hackamore 'em up, saddle 'em up, and get on' em and let 'em go. Sometimes he'd be too wild to pitch, he'd break and run, and you had to let 'em run himself down."

Tom Holland of Madisonville, Texas, was a teenage bronc buster and prided himself on his ability to train horses. He said, "I chopped cotton and plowed and split rails; then I was a horse rider. In them days, I could ride the wildest horse whatever made tracks in Texas….I'd make a dollar or fifty cents to ride wild horses in slavery time, and 'massa' let me keep it. I buyed tobacco and candy, and if 'massa' cotch me with tobacco, I'd get a whippin."

James Cape was trained to ride horses and tend cattle as a youngster in southeastern Texas. His owner sent him and four other slave children into Mexico to steal horses. They managed to get away with a herd of two hundred, and James was leading when they were caught in a terrible hailstorm. The children kept the herd together, and when they got home, the master was pleased and rewarded James with a new saddle. When the Civil War began, James's master sent him into the Confederate army to tend horses. He was shot in the shoulder and sent home. After the war, he worked for several different cattlemen in Texas and Missouri.

Some slaves were well trusted and given a lot of responsibility. Daniel Waggoner, a wealthy cattleman, bought a twelve-year-old Black boy who became his "young helper." They drove a large herd of cattle two hundred miles to their new home in Texas. During the Civil War, when Waggoner took cattle to Louisiana to sell to the Confederacy, he left his ranch and remaining herd in the care of this trusted young Black slave.

EARLY TRAIL DRIVES

While Texans were fighting for their freedom from Mexico in 1836, enterprising cattlemen were driving their longhorns to New Orleans or sending them down the Mississippi on steamships to the Crescent City. The first large cattle drive north from Texas was made in 1846 by Edward Piper, who took one thousand head to Ohio and sold them for a profit. Others drove herds to Ohio, Kentucky, and Pennsylvania, but the best markets were in Chicago and New York.

New markets in the West followed the 1848 California Gold Rush. A few bold stockmen drove cattle to San Francisco to supply the hungry prospectors and miners, but the distance and Indian attacks ended this venture. Sturdy longhorns were sold to pull the wagons of pioneers headed west on the California and Oregon Trails, while Santa Fe traders bought large numbers of them to pull their heavy wagons, loaded with trade goods. Large herds of longhorns were purchased by the army to supply troops building forts and protecting travelers and for railroad construction crews on the High Plains.

During the 1840s and 1850s, cattle headed for northern markets followed a route established by Indians, traders, and settlers coming to Texas from the Midwest. This was the Texas Road, later known as the Shawnee Trail, which crossed the Red River, Indian Territory, and split into branches to St. Louis, Sedalia, and several Kansas railheads.

The longhorns headed for market carried Texas Fever and passed it on to herds in Kansas and Missouri. Longhorns developed an immunity to the disease, but when midwestern cattle used a pasture where longhorns had been held, they became ill and died. In 1858, a terrible outbreak of Texas Fever left thousands of cattle dead, and many farmers lost their entire herds. In 1861, Missouri and the eastern counties of Kansas passed quarantine laws banning Texas longhorns. No one understood what caused Texas Fever or why it disappeared in the winter, but longhorn cattle spread it. A solution wasn't found until the 1890s, when scientific research proved that cattle ticks carried microbes that caused Texas Fever. Around 1917, the disease was finally controlled by a vigorous program of cattle dipping to eradicate ticks.

In 1859, the Pike's Peak Gold Rush drew thousands of hopefuls west, and by 1860, the Rockies were swarming with prospectors and miners, hungry for beef. Oliver Loving, a Texas cattleman, and three other ranchers drove their combined herd of 1,500 longhorns through Indian Territory and up the Arkansas River to Denver and sold them for thousands in gold dust.

The Civil War had just started, so Loving, a resident of a secessionist state, wasn't allowed to leave the Colorado Territory for several months. Finally, after the intercession of his influential friends—rancher John Iliff, landowner Lucien Maxwell, traders William Bent and Ceran St. Vrain, and Kit Carson—army officials let him leave. Loving headed back to Texas with his box of gold dust hidden beneath his wagon seat. Fearing robbers, he wore old, dusty clothes and drove a mismatched team with one large horse and one small. After three months on the road, he arrived in Texas, where Comanches had driven his family to safety in town.

The Union blockade of Southern ports stopped the shipment of longhorns to the Confederacy, cutting off income for Texas cattlemen. The price of longhorns dropped dramatically to two dollars per head as the cattle business fell apart. Disastrous droughts wiped out 75 percent of the cattle in worst-hit areas. During the Civil War, cattle drifted away from small ranches because there were no fences to contain them and no one to watch the herds. Cattle roamed the plains and vanished into the brush, where they continued to multiply. About 32 percent of small ranchers had a few cattle but did not own any slaves to care for them.

During the Civil War, Texans had little defense against the Comanches, who killed about 10 percent of the population and captured hundreds of women and children. Texans were also attacked by Kansas Jayhawkers and Comancheros from New Mexico, while epidemics of typhus and smallpox ravaged the exhausted population.

In 1865, the Confederacy surrendered, and the war finally ended. Cattlemen, who had managed to get through the seaport blockades or risked death driving herds to New Orleans, had wallets full of worthless

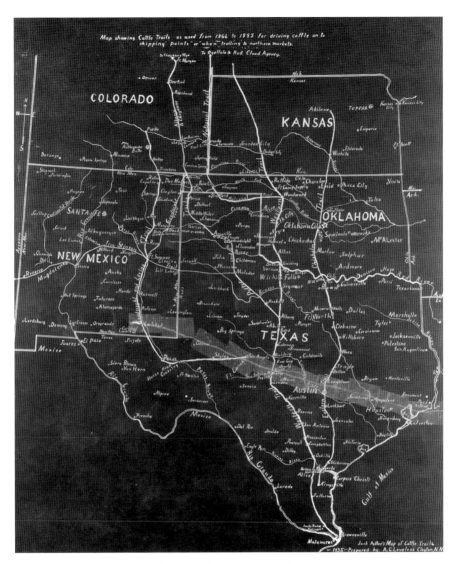

A 1935 map showing cattle trails as used from 1866 to 1895. *Via Texas History, https:// texashistory.unt.edu/ark:/67531/metapth493278, University of North Texas Libraries, The Portal to Texas History, Hardin-Simmons University Library.*

Confederate money. Many had been killed in the Civil War, and the slave population was sparse in the cow country. There were few men to ride the range or manage cattle, and Texas was overrun by about 5 million to 6 million longhorns. One-third of these animals were unbranded and became the quarry of Confederate army veterans rebuilding their herds with a long

Herding cattle. *Library of Congress.*

rope and a hot branding iron. A steer that was worth about four dollars in Texas sold for about forty dollars in the northern markets. The problem was getting the steers to market. More than 250,000 steers were driven up the Shawnee Trail toward Kansas and Missouri in 1866, but farmers, afraid of Texas Fever, turned them back.

The solution to the problem was the completion of the Kansas Pacific Railroad, but little progress was made during the war due to lack of materials and labor. Once the war ended, work on the railroad resumed, and the line advanced into Kansas. Stricter quarantine laws in Missouri and Kansas pushed Texas cattlemen farther west to an old trail that Indian trader Jesse Chisholm widened so his large wagons could use it. Chisholm owned trading posts in Kansas and Indian Territory, and cattlemen began calling this route "Chisholm's Trail."

In 1867, Joseph McCoy, a far-sighted businessman, saw the cattlemen's need for a permanent railhead where they could ship their herds to market. He persuaded Kansas Pacific executives to run a rail line into Abilene, a dilapidated settlement of scattered log shacks. This was west of the settled portion of Kansas, with its farmers and quarantine laws, and would be an ideal shipping point for cattlemen. McCoy built stock pens by the railroad tracks, opened a bank, and built a hotel for cattlemen.

McCoy advertised this new shipping depot throughout Texas and sent salesmen to meet cattlemen on the trail to convince them to bring their herds to Abilene. The first year, more than thirty-six thousand head of cattle were shipped to market from this railhead, and by 1868, about seventy-five thousand Texas longhorns had come up the Chisholm Trail to Abilene. Within five years, more than 3 million head of cattle were shipped. As the railroad built farther west in the 1870s, Ellsworth, Kansas, became a major shipping point. By 1880, Dodge City had captured much of the cattle trade, shipping more than 6 million head of cattle and helping to revive the Texas economy. This was the beginning of the era of the great cattle drives.

GOODNIGHT AND LOVING MAKE PLANS

Charles Goodnight knew that there was a market for cattle at Bosque Redondo, New Mexico, where nine thousand Navajos and Mescalero Apaches were imprisoned. The Indians were starving, and as conditions deteriorated, there was increased suffering, disease, and death at the internment camp. The military at nearby Fort Sumner was eager to buy beef to feed the Indians, and any cattle that they didn't purchase could be sold in the Colorado mining districts.

Goodnight had returned from the Civil War after protecting the border with the Texas Rangers and found most of his longhorns gone. He had no slaves to prevent the cattle from wandering off, and many had been stolen by Indians. Goodnight had to rebuild his herd, and the only way he could do this was to drive longhorns out of the brush.

By the spring of 1865, he had 1,200 cattle collected and was preparing for the drive to New Mexico when Indians ran off the entire bunch. Goodnight and a group of cowboys chased the raiding party twenty-five miles before deciding to turn back. Discouraged by this sorry state of affairs, he began once again. Despite Indians stealing his horses and killing some of the cowboys, Goodnight had gathered another herd by the spring of 1866 and once again prepared for his first cattle drive.

Goodnight had known hard times since he was a young boy in Illinois when his father died. He and his older brother had to support his mother and six siblings by splitting rails and working for neighboring farmers. When Goodnight was sixteen, he landed a job driving freight teams.

Image of a circa 1880 photo of cattleman Charles Goodnight. *University of North Texas Libraries, The Portal to Texas History, Cattle Raisers Museum.*

In 1853, their mother married a preacher, and Goodnight formed a partnership with his new stepbrother raising cattle. He continued working as a teamster, and instead of wages, he was paid in calves and gradually accumulated a small herd. While hauling freight, Goodnight met Oliver Loving, who'd brought his family from Kentucky to Texas in 1843. He farmed, hauled freight, and operated a general store near Fort Belknap. Loving had fifteen to twenty slaves, and by 1857, he owned more than one thousand acres and a large herd of longhorns. In 1860, Loving took a herd to Colorado and sold it in Denver for a profit.

During the Civil War, Loving drove his cattle to New Orleans and sold them to the Confederacy, and when the war ended, he was owed around $250,000 in worthless Confederate money. He faced ruin like many Texas cattlemen who'd been paid with Confederate dollars.

Loving learned about Goodnight's plans to sell cattle to the military in New Mexico and saw an opportunity. He advised the younger man about the hazards of the trail and difficulties he would encounter. He suggested they combine their herds for the drive to Fort Sumner, and Goodnight quickly agreed. He was a seasoned Indian fighter, while Loving was an experienced trail driver and knew the dangers they'd face. He was fifty-four with a large family and older than Goodnight, a thirty-year-old bachelor.

To avoid Comanche-Kiowa Territory, Goodnight planned a longer, roundabout route, following the old Butterfield Mail Route across the North and Middle Concho Rivers. They'd push west across ninety-six miles of bleak, arid Llano Estacado (the Staked Plains). Crossing this wasteland without water was the most hazardous part of the journey and required three days and three nights. At the western end of the Staked Plains, they would pass through Castle Gap, a mile-long canyon in the flat-topped Castle Mountains. Water for the herd was twelve miles ahead at the treacherous Horsehead Crossing on the Pecos River. There they'd turn north toward the Rockies and follow the river to Fort Sumner.

Goodnight believed that his best opportunity to recruit top hands for the cattle drive was to provide plenty of good food cooked well and served on time. He knew that this was very important to cowboys, who were in the saddle twelve to sixteen hours every day. He decided that a mobile kitchen was needed, so he bought a used Studebaker wagon and designed the first chuck wagon.

Goodnight hired Frank Mayes, an emancipated slave, as cook for sixty dollars per month. Mayes had plenty of experience cooking on Loving's cattle drives to New Orleans. Goodnight would be the trail boss because he knew cattle and the plains and had plenty of experience fighting Indians.

Goodnight carefully hired the crew of eighteen skilled, dependable cowboys for the drive. There were several Black cowboys: Jim Fowler, who'd been on Loving's 1860 cattle drive to Denver; a young Black cowboy known only as Little Tom; Dan Sauls; and Bose Ikard. This was Bose's first cattle drive, but he'd been working for Loving since emancipation, after being highly recommended by Dr. Milton Ikard, a neighbor. Bose was born enslaved in Mississippi in 1847 and came to Texas when he was five years old with his father, Dr. Ikard. Bose took care of livestock and, as a teen, could rope and ride as well as any man.

White cowboys in the crew included "One-Arm Bill" Wilson and his brothers, Charles and LaFayette, who were Goodnight's friends; "Crosseyed" Nathan Brauner; John Bull; Jim Reynolds; and Clay Allison, a top hand before he became a notorious gunfighter in New Mexico.

Next to good cowhands, good horses were an important part of the trail outfit, and Goodnight had eighty-five horses and mules in his remuda. There were enough horses for each cowboy to have one to ride during the day, with one or two more that could be switched out so none of the animals became too tired. Each cowboy had at least one night horse, used only for guarding the herd at night.

GOODNIGHT AND LOVING BLAZE A TRAIL

Oliver Loving and Charles Goodnight combined their herds south of Fort Belknap near the Brazos River and headed west toward New Mexico on June 6, 1866. Their herd of two thousand cattle was driven by eighteen well-armed men, and they turned southwest following the route of the Butterfield Mail.

Goodnight was up before dawn, riding several miles ahead of the herd, looking for water holes and grass where the cattle could graze and rest at midday. Then he located a bedding-down place near water for the night. Goodnight assigned positions around the herd where each cowboy rode as the cattle moved along the trail. The point men rode in front, the swing men along the side, flankers toward the back, and the drag men brought up the rear. Each morning, everyone rotated except the point men, who kept their envied position at the front.

Goodnight and Loving were driving a mixed herd of steers, yearlings, cows, and calves. The steers moved along steadily and were easier to handle than cows, but they were more inclined to stampede. If a steer broke out of the line, the nearest cowboy had to chase him and bring him back. Usually, the same steer moved to the front of the herd every morning and led the cattle. On subsequent Goodnight drives, "Old Blue," a very large steer, always led the herd.

The cattle moved forward at a steady pace, strung out in a long line that often extended back for half a mile or more. The spread of their horns kept the cattle six to seven feet apart and prevented crowding and overheating.

The herd usually traveled about ten to fifteen miles a day, and the cattle became easier to manage the longer they were on the trail.

When they were traveling through Indian country, Goodnight and the others kept a watchful eye on the horizon. Comanches might swoop down from the hills at any time, stampede the cattle, and make off with as many as they could. Sometimes, they demanded payment in cattle for safe passage through their territory. Goodnight tried to keep the peace and usually gave the Indians a few animals, which was much easier than fighting them.

Cows that delivered their calves along the way were a problem because the wobbly newborns couldn't keep up with the others. Bawling cows looking for their lost calves slowed the entire herd, and there was no way to carry the young animals. Since a calf sold with a cow had no financial value, the usual solution was to shoot them. Goodnight recalled, "I always hated killing the little innocent things, but it had to be done as cows and calves slowed the herd." This terrible task fell to Black cowboy Jim Fowler, a former slave who called himself "Jim Goodnight." Upset by this heartless assignment, Jim finally asked Goodnight for a different job, saying, "I just don't like killing the little calfies!" Goodnight told him it had to be done, vowing that he'd never trail a mixed herd again. When they were near a ranch, Fowler happily traded the calves for fresh eggs and vegetables instead of killing them.

Following the Butterfield route, they passed forts abandoned when the Civil War began and reached Buffalo Gap. They drove the cattle across the North Concho and Middle Concho Rivers and then rested the herd. Arid land was ahead, so they let the cattle eat and drink their fill. The cowboys filled extra canteens, and Fred Mayes made sure that the water barrels on the chuck wagon were full. Then the cowboys on point turned west, and the herd moved out. Ahead lay ninety-six miles of waterless, barren desert, the Llano Estacado, the Staked Plains. They trailed the cattle across the hot, alkali flats all day, only stopping for a few hours in the middle of the night as the thirsty cattle milled around restlessly.

Goodnight pushed the herd back on the trail before dawn and decided to keep traveling night and day. The weary cattle plodded along the second day, urged ahead under the merciless sun. Clouds of white alkali dust choked the tired cowboys and irritated their eyes as they tried to quench their thirst with warm water from their canteens. Their throats burned, and their lips were dried out and cracked, but they knew that they had to make the water last as long as possible. There was no water for the suffering cattle and only small amounts for the horses.

The men on point held the cattle back, while the flankers tried to keep them bunched together. The pounds seemed to melt off the cattle, as they quickly lost weight; their ribs stuck out, their flanks were gaunt, and their eyes were sunken into their sockets. Exhausted animals dropped in their tracks, while others followed blindly and stumbled over the carcasses. Occasionally, a wild-eyed steer, tongue lolling out of his mouth, broke out of the herd in a futile, mad search for water. The cowboys let the frantic animal go, knowing that he was dead already.

By the third day, the suffering of both the men and the cattle was terrible, but they stumbled on. Wheezing and coughing, the cowboys' shouts and curses were lost in the din of the bawling, moaning cattle. Goodnight was everywhere—riding point, offering his canteen to a thirsty cowboy, moving to the rear, and encouraging the drag men who were pushing the weakest animals along.

The evening shadows brought some relief from the heat, and the stars glittered in the night sky. The chuck wagon was pulled to the front of the line, and as each exhausted cowboy passed, Frank Mayes handed him a cup of strong, black coffee. Around two o'clock in the morning, they reached Castle Gap, a mile-long canyon through the flat-topped Castle Mountains on the western edge of the Staked Plains. Horsehead Crossing of the Pecos River lay twelve miles ahead.

As the cattle moved forward through the narrow canyon, they caught a faint smell of water, and the thirst-crazed animals stampeded. Riding wildly, Goodnight, Wilson, Ikard, and the others managed to stop them, but as the cattle neared the Pecos, they became unmanageable again and frantically raced toward the water. Reaching the river, the lead cattle rushed down the steep bank, tumbled into the water as others followed and pushed them forward into the river. Soon the Pecos was filled bank to bank with thirsty, bawling cattle. Once the animals drank their fill and quenched their thirst, they were herded up the opposite bank to graze on thick grass. The riverbanks were littered with the bleached skulls and scattered bones of horses and mules that had died here after gulping too much of the briny water.

Some cattle were sinking into the river's treacherous quicksand, so everyone went to work trying to extract them. This was hard work, and exhausted cowboys flopped down in the grass for a few minutes' rest. They soon resumed the job of saving trapped, terrified cattle, but after three days at the backbreaking task, they had to move on, leaving behind hundreds wallowing in the deadly sand. No one got enough rest to stave off the overwhelming exhaustion, and Goodnight later said of this terrible river crossing, "The Pecos—the graveyard of a cowman's hopes. I hated it! It was as treacherous as the Indians themselves!" He calculated that he'd lost three hundred animals to thirst, drowning, and quicksand in the Pecos.

Goodnight said, "At that time, the Pecos was the most desolate country that I had ever explored. The river was full of fish, but besides the fish there was scarcely a living thing, not even wolves or birds." The bleak, forbidding country around the Pecos did have an abundance of rattlesnakes. Cowboy Nath Brauner, who was cross-eyed, killed all the snakes he could see, despite his defective vision. Since ammunition was hard for former Confederates to get after the Civil War, Goodnight told the men to not waste bullets, but Brauner apparently had plenty because he blazed away to his heart's content. He kept seventy-two rattles to send home to his mother in Kentucky and bragged that his eye problem gave him an advantage since he could watch the herd with one eye and shoot rattlesnakes with the other!

They pushed on toward Fort Sumner, finally reached Pope's Crossing on the Pecos, and forded the river safely. They moved along the west side of the Pecos past the present site of Carlsbad, New Mexico, and wasted no time pushing the herd through Apache territory to Fort Sumner. The fort had been built in 1864 to guard the Navajos who'd made the terrible "Long Walk" from their home in Arizona to this reservation-prison. The partners sold their steers to the army for the high price of eight cents per pound on the hoof and were elated at getting so much money. They were paid $12,000 in gold and decided to sell the remaining cows and calves in Colorado.

They rested a few days before heading north, and Frank Mayes cooked up a fine holiday meal to celebrate the Fourth of July. They feasted on light sourdough biscuits, ribs, and a pot of son of a gun stew that Mayes had put on to cook the previous night. The cowboys knew that their cook was in a good mood when he brought out fragrant fruit pies for dessert. Pleasantly stuffed, everyone lounged around the campfire, smoking and telling tale tales.

The next morning, Oliver Loving, One-Arm Bill Wilson, Frank Mayes, Little Tom, and Jim Fowler set off from Fort Sumner driving the herd of eight hundred cows and calves to Colorado. They traveled up the Pecos to Las Vegas and then followed the Santa Fe Trail west to Raton Pass. Loving paid Uncle Dick Wooten's toll of ten cents per head to cross the pass, and they pushed past Trinidad, around the base of the Rockies to Pueblo, and on to Denver. Loving sold all the cattle to John Iliff, a Denver merchant who was establishing a large ranch on the eastern Colorado plains.

Photo from the U.S. Army Signal Corps. Navajo captives from the Long Walk receive rations under guard at Bosque Redondo, Fort Sumner, New Mexico, in the 1860s. *Palace of the Governors Photo Archive Negative Number 028536.*

While Loving was headed toward Denver, Goodnight started back to Texas with Bose Ikard and two other cowboys. He gave Ikard the $12,000 in gold, and the cowboy hid it in his bedroll, tucked behind his saddle. Provisions for the journey were loaded on a pack mule, and they left the army post, traveling at night to avoid being seen by Apaches. A thunderstorm struck on a dangerous part of the trail, with fierce lightning and booming thunder, but they pushed on, stumbling through sheets of blinding rain and howling wind. A sudden clap of thunder frightened the pack mule, and he broke away and raced off into the darkness. Goodnight chased him and managed to catch the mule's rope and hang on while the animal bucked wildly and did his best to get loose. Somehow Goodnight managed to bring the mule to a standstill, but all the food supplies had been tossed far and wide in the melee. The men scrambled around in the darkness and soaking rain trying unsuccessfully to find anything they could eat. When morning came, the hungry cowboys searched again but found only one small piece of bacon. The coyotes had discovered their lost supplies and carried everything away—even the tobacco! They were five hundred miles from anywhere, in the middle of dangerous Apache country. They spent the day hungry, hiding from the Indians until darkness fell and then moved on.

In addition to hunger, Goodnight was miserable with an earache, fever, and a nasty cold. His hearing was already impaired as a complication of measles that he'd contracted in the Texas Rangers. Now he could hardly hear at all—a dangerous problem when trying to pass through country that was crawling with Apaches and rattlesnakes! Years later, Goodnight recalled, "Every once in a while, the boys would yell, 'Look out Charlie, there's another rattler. I didn't know which way to jump!'"

They were afraid to shoot a rabbit because a gunshot could bring the Indians, and turning back wasn't an option. When they reached Horsehead Crossing, they filled their canteens with alkali water and started across the forbidding Llano Estacado. As they plodded along, they saw figures on the eastern horizon that could be Indians. Knowing they were goners, they prepared for the worst. Although Goodnight's illness had compromised his hearing, he had exceptional vision, and he watched closely as the figures came nearer. As Ikard and the others prepared for a fight, Goodnight suddenly gave a whoop. This wasn't Indians! Instead, six mules pulling a large wagon loaded with watermelons was approaching them! The driver was an older settler who'd decided to sell his melons to Mexicans who came to the nearby salt lakes to get cartloads of salt. Goodnight assured the melon farmer that he had a ready market right in front of him as the hungry cowboys crowded around the wagon. The juicy melons were sliced and gobbled, and watermelon never tasted as good as it did that day. The settler gave them enough provisions to get them home, so they made the rest of their journey without incident.

Years later, Goodnight recalled their desperate situation and said, "I learned a lesson that I would never forget....I thought to myself, here you are with more gold than you ever had in your life, and it won't buy you a drink of water, and it won't get you food. For this gold you may have led three men to their death—for a thing that is utterly useless to you. I never got over the impression that made on me, and I believe it is one reason I've never worshipped money since."

Goodnight was anxious to return to New Mexico to sell another herd to the military before the first snows. It had taken his group seventeen days to return to Texas, riding about forty miles per day. Within twelve days, Goodnight had a crew with Bose Ikard, Jim Fowler, One-Arm Bill Wilson, and Frank Mayes and 900 head of cattle, and they'd driven the herd west to the Brazos River. Here 1,200 longhorns were added to the herd. They were on their way when the herd was split apart by the sudden

Goodnight-Loving Trail historical marker in New Mexico. *Bill Kirchner via the Historical Marker Database, hmdb.org.*

rush of a buffalo stampede. The cowboys rode it out, rounded up their cattle, and reassembled the herd, pleased that they hadn't lost any animals. Before they reached the arid Llano Estacado, they rested the cattle where there was plenty of grass and water. They were in better condition and crossed the desert and the treacherous river without losing one animal!

Forty days after leaving Texas, they reached Bosque Grande ("large forest" in Spanish). Loving was waiting after selling the cows and calves in Denver, so they had reason to celebrate. Frank Mayes cooked up another fine meal while the men relaxed, knowing that they'd made two difficult cattle drives in a very short time. Goodnight and Loving formed a partnership, built corrals, and made dugout dwellings by burrowing into the bluffs along the river. They spent a comfortable winter of 1866–67 in their primitive prairie homes and drove one hundred cattle to Santa Fe monthly, sold them, and bought supplies for their Bosque Redondo ranch.

TRAGEDY STRIKES IN 1867

In the spring of 1867, Goodnight and Loving drove the cattle from Bosque Grande to Denver and sold them. Then they returned to Texas, anxious to gather another herd of longhorns and drive them back to New Mexico. The start of this third drive in June 1867 was slowed by heavy rains, stampedes, and threats of Indian attacks. Goodnight, a great believer in intuition and "hunches," recalled years later that they were hoping for a peaceful, profitable return drive to New Mexico, but "the signs weren't quite right."

They'd barely started the drive when they were attacked during the night by Comanches, who drove off part of the herd. Goodnight and Bose Ikard trailed the stolen cattle about fifteen miles, recovered them, and drove them back to camp. The following night, they were attacked again by Comanches, who drove off most of the horses. Goodnight chased them for miles, and the Comanches fled, abandoning the animals.

During this raid, a young cowboy, Long Joe Loving (no relation to Oliver), was hit by an arrow, and its iron tip was lodged firmly in his skull behind his ear. Goodnight knew that this would have to be removed, but it would be a delicate, dangerous job. His only surgical instrument was a pair of "old-fashioned shoe pliers." Years later, Goodnight recalled, "Two strong men held Joe down, and I succeeded in pulling the arrow out with the pinchers." The cowboy was loaded into a wagon and driven miles back to the Goodnight ranch, where the cattleman's mother took care of him until he recovered.

The cattle stampeded again, and another day was spent rounding them up. Since there were so many Indians determined to steal the horses or cattle, Loving and Goodnight decided to leave the area quickly. They pushed the herd onto the trail in a heavy rain and hadn't gone far before the animals stampeded a third time. Intense lightning slashed across the dark sky, and thunder boomed. As the cowboys raced alongside the cattle, their horses' hooves struck sparks on the rocks, and the electricity in the air sent tiny flames darting around the horses' ears. Flashes of lightning revealed wild-eyed cattle with balls of fire dancing above their horns. Goodnight recalled, "I had placed two first-class men, Bose Ikard and Dan Sauls, on the corners of the herd in the rear and took One-Arm Bill Wilson and went on the point myself." They managed to finally stop the stampede and get the cattle milling together in a large circle. They endured a miserable night soaked by sheets of heavy rain, while the wind blew a gale. The storm finally moved on, and the exhausted cowboys rolled up in their blankets for a little sleep until morning.

The following day was spent rounding up runaways and watching for Indians. Goodnight praised his men for their work and quietly told Bose that he was one of the best cowboys he'd ever ridden with on a night stampede and that he'd "handled himself well!" As they moved ahead, the partners counted their cattle and found that they'd lost several hundred head in the stampede. When they reached Horsehead Crossing on the Pecos, they saw a large party of Indians with several hundred of their cattle. Deciding that it was impossible to recover the animals and anxious to keep their scalps, Goodnight and Loving pushed the herd across the Pecos quickly and headed for Fort Sumner.

It was the end of June, and Loving was anxious to get their bid for a beef contract in before the approaching deadline; he said he was going ahead to Fort Sumner alone. Goodnight tried to convince him that this was dangerous because of the numerous bands of Comanches and Apaches roaming the region. Loving was stubbornly undeterred but agreed to let Bill Wilson go with him. Goodnight advised them to travel at night and hide in the daytime so they wouldn't be seen by war parties.

Years later, Goodnight described Oliver Loving as "one of the coolest and bravest men I have ever known but devoid of caution." He later learned that Loving and Wilson traveled after dark only the first two nights. Then Loving became very impatient, insisting that they ignore Goodnight's "overly cautious" advice and move on during the day. Wilson finally gave in, and on the third day, they crossed the Pecos and were traveling north through open country when eight Comanches galloped toward them. They quickly turned back toward the Pecos, where there was brushy cover.

The group of eight Comanches grew into a huge war party of four to five hundred warriors who gave chase. When Loving and Wilson reached the river, they spurred their horses down a steep bluff, dismounted quickly, and scrambled for cover in some stunted bushes. The Indians swarmed down the riverbank, seized their horses, hid in tall reeds, and moved closer. Warriors on the bluff above showered them with arrows, and suddenly an Indian jumped up near Loving and shot him. The bullet tore through Loving's left wrist, breaking the bone, and plowed into his left side. Wilson drove back a fierce Comanche charge as Loving crawled to a hiding place in a sandy depression beneath the overhanging riverbank. The Indians kept up their sporadic attacks, sending hundreds of arrows over the bluff, while Wilson held them off with rifle fire.

The hours crawled by, and daylight waned as Loving, weakened from the loss of blood, developed a fever. Wilson, who was watching for Comanches, saw another brave creeping closer through the reeds, but suddenly the sharp buzzing of a hidden rattlesnake made him quickly back away.

When darkness fell, Wilson crept quietly to the river and filled his boot with water to quench Loving's thirst. As time dragged by, fever-wracked Loving became convinced that he was going to die and that Wilson would eventually be killed by the Indians. He pleaded with Wilson to escape, to find Goodnight and tell his family what had happened. Loving insisted that he could hold off the Comanches and would never be taken alive. He said if the Indians left, he would crawl to the river, swim downstream a few miles, and hide until Wilson and Goodnight returned.

Wilson doubted that this would work but finally agreed to go for help. He arranged five six-shooters and a rifle within Loving's reach and, at his insistence, agreed to take Loving's new sixteen-shot Henry repeating rifle. When the moon went down and the night was black, Wilson clasped Loving's hand farewell and slipped away into the darkness. At the river's edge, he removed his boots and most of his clothes; wearing only his hat and underwear, he eased quietly into the stream. He hid his clothes underwater where the Indians wouldn't find them and drifted slowly downstream. A watchful Comanche was sitting on a horse midstream, posted to prevent his escape. Wilson quietly moved toward the riverbank, where he was concealed by weeds and overhanging bushes. As he inched along, he was suddenly swept into deep water, which carried him safely past the Indian lookout.

Portrait of Oliver Loving, who blazed the Goodnight-Loving Trail with Charles Goodnight in 1866. *Public domain.*

Wilson tried to swim downstream with his one arm burdened by the heavy rifle and almost drowned three times. He finally hid the rifle underwater, covered by sand so the Indians wouldn't find it. Then he drifted quietly past the Comanches camped on the riverbank above and swam until he could safely climb out of the water. He hid in a canebrake all day, and as darkness fell, he began walking barefoot across the rocks and gravel hills along the Pecos. He was sure that Goodnight and the herd would be coming along the cattle trail soon.

Unfortunately, Goodnight had stopped to rest the herd for two days, so rescue was much farther away than Wilson thought. He hid during the hot daylight hours and limped on at night. Later, in recounting his ordeal, Wilson said, "Everything in that country had stickers. On my way, I picked up the small end of a tepee pole which I used for a walking stick. The last night of this painful journey, the wolves followed me all night. I would give out, just like a horse, and lay down in the road and drop off to sleep, and when I would awaken the wolves would be all around me, snapping and snarling. I would take up that stick, knock the wolves away, get started again, and the wolves would follow behind. I kept that up until daylight when the wolves quit me. About noon on that last day, I crossed a little mountain and knew the boys ought to be right in there somewhere with the cattle. I found a little place, a sort of cave, that offered protection from the sun and I could go no further. After a time, the boys came along with the cattle and found me."

When he was riding ahead of the herd, Goodnight saw a figure emerge from a cave about a quarter of a mile away, waving his arms and beckoning to him. He said later, "Whether it was intuition or a sixth sense, I knew positively it was Wilson, and how, I knew I will never understand!" Goodnight galloped up to Wilson, who was so overcome by emotion he was unable to speak. Goodnight said, "He was the most terrible object I ever saw! His eyes were wild and bloodshot, his feet were swollen beyond all reason, and every step he took left blood in the track. I inquired about Loving, but he could scarcely make a reply, and what he did mutter was entirely unintelligible. I put him on my horse and got him to my herd as soon as possible, which his brother had already got together for action. I tore up a blanket, wet it, wrapped his feet to remove the fever, and then Frank made him a light gruel of meal which I gave him at intervals for almost an hour. By then he was perfectly himself. I asked him for particulars, and he told me in detail of their trip and the attack by Indians."

Anxious to save Loving if possible, Goodnight, Bose Ikard, and five cowboys headed for the Pecos that evening. They rode all night through a rain so heavy that at times they were forced to stop because they couldn't see. They reached the river the next day and found Loving's hiding place, but he was gone. They searched downriver, where Loving had said he would go, but the heavy rain had washed away all tracks or sign of him. Goodnight reluctantly decided that Loving had killed himself to avoid Indian capture, and his body had drifted downstream. Wilson had described where he hid his clothes and Loving's Henry rifle so accurately that Goodnight found everything without difficulty. The group searched the area for Loving until darkness fell and then, convinced that he was dead, sadly made their way back to the herd.

Weeks later, as they moved up the Pecos, Goodnight was scouting ahead for signs of Indians when he met a cattleman who gave him the good news that Loving was alive at Fort Sumner. He had been taken to the fort in a wagon by several Mexicans. The cattleman said that Loving had managed to hold off the Comanches for two days and nights. Then he crawled into the river and swam upstream instead of downstream as planned, thinking that he'd have a better chance of being found by travelers.

When Loving reached the Pecos crossing, he'd hidden nearby for two days. He was so hungry that he tried to eat his leather gloves but couldn't get a fire started to roast them. He tried to shoot birds in the nearby trees, but his gunpowder was wet. He grew so weak from hunger that he wasn't able to crawl down the riverbank to get water, so he tied his scarf to a stick, wet it in the river, and sucked the moisture out.

Three days after reaching the river crossing, Loving was only semi-conscious when he was found by a young boy gathering wood. He was with a group of Mexicans with a wagon who were traveling east to Texas. They cared for Loving and hauled him 150 miles to Fort Sumner.

Goodnight could hardly believe the cattleman's story about Loving's rescue and quickly saddled Jenny, his surefooted mule, and left the herd in Wilson's hands. The one-armed cowboy was recovering from his ordeal, knew the trail, and would manage the drive from his wagon seat.

Goodnight hadn't gotten much sleep for the past thirty-two days and nights, so he dozed fitfully in the saddle as Jenny, surefooted and easy gaited, steadily covered the miles. When he reached Fort Sumner the following night, he learned that Loving had been walking about, and the wound in his side was healed. However, an infection had developed in his wounded arm, and the post's young army surgeon was hoping to avoid an amputation, an operation that he had never performed. The fort's older, more experienced surgeon was in Santa Fe and wasn't available to help. Goodnight became increasingly alarmed as gangrene spread though Loving's arm, and he developed a generalized infection. As his condition deteriorated, Goodnight told the young surgeon "briefly and in no uncertain words that he 'must take the arm off!'" The doctor finally agreed and amputated Loving's left arm above the elbow, but the patient developed bleeding complications the day after the operation. Using relays of horses, Goodnight sent a messenger to a doctor in Las Vegas, asking him to come to Fort Sumner as quickly as possible. He included $500 "for expenses" with this urgent request.

Two physicians responded and stopped the bleeding, but without modern antibiotics, Loving's condition continued to deteriorate over the following twenty-two days. Aware that he was failing, Loving asked Goodnight to continue their business partnership for the next two years until his debts were paid and his family was financially secure. He regretted being buried "in a foreign country," and Goodnight promised that his body would "be laid in a cemetery at home." Oliver Loving died at Fort Sumner on September 25, 1867, and was temporarily buried there.

Site of the home of Oliver Loving in 1855, Texas Centennial historical marker in Palo Pinto County, Texas. *Larry D. Moore, CC BY-SA 4.0, via Wikimedia Commons.*

After Loving's burial, the grief-stricken Goodnight headed back down the trail and brought the herd to Fort Sumner. Since he'd missed the contract deadline, he took the cattle north to Colorado. It was in the fall of 1867 when his cowboys pushed the cattle through the high mesas of the Raton Range, across the Continental Divide to Uncle Dick Wooten's toll station at Raton Pass. It cost ten cents per animal to cross, and when Goodnight protested that this was too much, Wooten refused to lower the rate or give him a discount. Goodnight furiously swore to find another pass and blaze a new trail while Wooten laughed in his face and sneered that there was no other pass. Goodnight angrily paid the toll, but as the herd headed toward Trinidad, he swore that Dick Wooten would pay.

From the top of Raton Pass, the Texas cowboys could see Colorado and a vast valley far to the north, rimmed by the Spanish Peaks, Greenhorn Mountain, and Pike's Peak. The foothills rolled away to a great plateau covered with deep grass and broken up by scattered canyons. Several streams cut across this plateau, flowing north toward the Arkansas River. Goodnight decided to establish a swing ranch in Apishapa Canyon, forty miles east of Trinidad. There was water, and the walls of the twenty-mile-long canyon would shelter the cattle and horses during the winter. The cattle were turned loose, and the cowboys started building a cabin. Goodnight rode five hundred miles back to New Mexico to meet Jim Loving, Oliver's twenty-one-year-old son, who'd just brought a large herd from Texas to Bosque Grande.

Young Loving had lost more than one thousand longhorns in stampedes, stolen by the Indians, or dead from thirst on this drive. Most of the cattle were in poor condition, but Goodnight cut out about one thousand head that were in the best shape and prepared to drive them to Colorado. His crew was experienced and included Black cowboys Jim Fowler, Bose Ikard,

Cowboy rounding up cattle circa 1902. *Public domain.*

Dan Sauls, and Frank Mayes. The drive north was miserable, as winter had set in early, and a blizzard howled over the mountains. The cattle and horses struggled through deep snow on Raton Pass and reached Apishapa on Christmas Eve 1867. The cowboys whooped, turned the herd loose for the winter, and headed for the warmth of the new cabin.

In just one season, the Goodnight-Loving Trail had become an important route, with numerous cattlemen following it to Fort Sumner and north into Colorado and Wyoming. Eventually, in the 1870s, some Texas drovers took this trail through southern New Mexico around the Apache stronghold in the Guadalupe Mountains and west to deliver cattle to the new Apache reservations in Arizona.

THE GOODNIGHT-LOVING TRAIL
BRINGS CATTLEMEN WEST

John Hittson watched from a hill as Charles Goodnight and Oliver Loving began their cattle drive from Texas to New Mexico in June 1866. He wanted to take advantage of the lucrative market with the army at Fort Sumner too. An impoverished southerner, he'd left Tennessee seeking opportunity in Texas before the Civil War, but life wasn't easy. Hittson had built a cattle herd by chasing wild longhorns out of the brush and branding unmarked animals. He often went months without sleeping under a roof, and his body was scarred from battles with Indians.

John Hittson and his brother William didn't own slaves, and it was dangerous in Texas to speak out against slavery. From 1861 to 1863, the Hittsons avoided Confederate authorities, who were drafting men between ages eighteen and forty-five to serve in the Rebel forces. To feed their families during the war, they took herds across the Rio Grande, sold them in Mexico, and traded salt and dried beef for food and supplies. Both activities were forbidden by the Confederacy, but the tough Hittsons took their chances.

Hittson prepared for the cattle drive to New Mexico and hired additional cowboys, including formerly enslaved men Mel Johnson and Louis Callahan. These reliable men were top hands who'd worked with him for several years. Eight wagons carrying twenty well-armed Texans, who planned to settle in New Mexico, would accompany this cattle drive. Their guns would provide additional protection on the desolate Llano Estacado, where roaming Comanches and Apaches often attacked travelers. Preparing for that arid wasteland, Hittson included an extra wagon loaded with barrels of water for the men and horses. There would be no relief for the cattle until they reached the Pecos. Before the end of June 1866, Hittson's caravan and cattle moved out of Palo Pinto County following Goodnight and Loving's trail.

They made good progress, and when they reached the alkali flats of Llano Estacado, Hittson pushed the herd forward night and day without stopping. He knew that some Goodnight-Loving cattle died after gulping the poisonous alkaline water from ponds near Horsehead Crossing, so he avoided the treacherous crossing and turned his herd north toward Pope's Crossing. Here they were able to water the cattle and get the herd across the Pecos safely, and then they traveled along the west bank of the river to Bosque Redondo.

Hittson, Callahan, Johnson, and the crew were on the trail for three months, arriving in August 1866. All the cattle were sold to the army for a good profit, except for one hundred that Hittson sold at Fort Union. Their Texan companions and their wagons continued on the Mountain Branch of the Santa Fe Trail to the Canadian River, where they settled. They built log cabins and a hotel, the Clifton House, which soon became a stop for the southbound stage from Colorado.

Hittson sold most of their horses in New Mexico, and Mel Johnson, Lewis Callahan, and the other cowboys piled into an oxen-drawn wagon and headed back to Texas. Near the Pecos River, the Indians had left a gruesome warning for them: a white man's head impaled on a pole. Smoke signals rose from the surrounding hills as they neared the Middle Concho River, where they were attacked by Kiowas. The cowboys grabbed their muzzle loaders, jumped out of the wagon, and took refuge under the overhanging riverbank. After firing a few shots, the Indians began laughing, stopped shooting, and rode off, taking the wagon, oxen, and their only two saddle horses.

It was eighty miles to home, so Hittson and the others began walking. It was winter, and they had no food or blankets. They walked at night to avoid Indians and hid in the daytime, burrowing into snowbanks and huddling together to keep warm. Four days before Christmas 1866, the hungry, half-frozen group limped into the tiny settlement at Fort Davis, Texas. After four days of recuperation, Hittson rounded the cowboys up, insisting that they all accompany him back to the place where they were attacked. Everyone was surprised to find the wagon there, still in one piece, and their oxen alive.

Back home in Palo Pinto County, everyone was excited about the success of Hittson's cattle drive. Fueled by dreams of New Mexico gold, other cattlemen rounded up and branded every four-legged critter that was hiding in the brush and prepared to head west.

After this first successful cattle drive, Hittson made many more, delivering about eight thousand longhorns per year to New Mexico and Colorado. He bought rich grazing land southeast of Denver near Deer Trail, Colorado, and in 1872 he moved his Texas cattle operation to his new Six Springs Ranch there. He had a crew of fifty experienced cowboys, including Mel Johnson and Louis Callahan, to herd longhorns on the new ranch.

Little is known about Mel Johnson, who was born enslaved, but Lewis Callahan's father had taken his owner's name and, when emancipated, moved his family to Texas. Lewis drove freight wagons as a teen, and his excellent reputation was helpful in getting him work as a teamster on wagon trains to Oregon, California, and Colorado.

Lewis married and settled down in 1888 and homesteaded near Deer Trail. He and his wife, Alice, eventually owned more than two thousand acres and were respected cattle ranchers. They raised brood mares and fast quarter horses that often captured first place at the Cheyenne Frontier Days races.

The Deer Trail Pioneer Historical Society wrote in *A History of Deer Trail*, "The Callahans were well-liked, it was always a pleasure to visit their home." They were often referred to as "Aunt Alice" and "Uncle Lewis." Despite this friendly acceptance, the Callahans experienced some racial prejudice. Lewis had quietly acquired stock in the Deer Trail Bank, but when it had financial problems, he wasn't invited to the bank's board meeting. When he tried to attend, the door was slammed in his face. Furious, Lewis immediately opened an account at a rival Denver bank and transferred all his money. Within three days, the Deer Trail Bank had closed its doors because it no longer had enough funds to operate.

Lewis Callahan developed a blood clot after hernia surgery and died in 1923. He survived John Hittson, who was thrown from a runaway wagon and broke his neck on Christmas Day 1880. Hittson, who was nicknamed "Cattle Jack," built a cattle empire and was just forty-nine when he died.

While Hittson was building an empire of longhorns, Goodnight was driving himself relentlessly. Worried about his debts as well as those of Loving, he and his crew worked without stopping. Once a herd was delivered in New Mexico or Colorado, they'd head back to Texas to pick up another. Determined to deliver cattle on the contract date but uncertain of the calendar day, arguments about this were always settled by Bose Ikard, since Goodnight, like most cattlemen, believed that Black cowboys never lost track of time or the date.

Goodnight delivered large mixed herds to John Iliff, who was establishing his cattle empire and wanted cows and calves. Goodnight built a wagon to carry forty calves, and now, instead of shooting the newborns, Jim Fowler picked them up when they were "dropped" and drove this "blattin wagon." Every morning, the bedding ground was full of anxious cows fussing over their tiny calves that had been born during the night. Cows recognized their calves by their scent, and when their babies were piled in the wagon together, their scents became mixed, so the cows could no longer identify their own offspring. Goodnight came up with the idea of numbering each calf, putting it in a sack with a matching number for the daytime wagon ride. This kept the calves' scents separated, and in the evening, at the bedding spot, the calves were taken out of their bags, after which the cows quickly found their babies. The calves spent the night with their mothers and then were "bagged up" in the morning and loaded in the wagon. After a few days, most calves were strong enough to keep up with the herd and no longer needed a ride.

In the spring of 1868, Goodnight drove the first herd of Texas longhorns into Wyoming, extending the Goodnight-Loving Trail from southern New Mexico through Colorado into Wyoming Territory. Cattle drovers from Texas soon ventured farther north into the Montana grasslands and east into Dakota Territory.

Goodnight began taking his herds farther east to avoid Dick Wooten's toll station on Raton Pass and discovered Trinchera Pass. This was a more

Goodnight-Loving Trail marker. The Goodnight-Loving cattle trail was blazed by Charles Goodnight and Oliver Loving in 1866 from Texas to New Mexico, north through Colorado. It was extended into Wyoming in 1867. *F.J. Athearn, Bureau of Land Management, from Land of Contrast: A History of Southeast Colorado, BLM Cultural Resources Series (Colorado: No. 17).*

gradual grade into Colorado and turned north to the Picket Wire River (the Purgatory) and east toward Grenada, Colorado. Now it was Goodnight's turn to laugh at Dick Wooten, because he had found another pass into Colorado, and there was no toll to pay! As the cattleman continued to drive herds farther east to avoid Raton Pass, others followed, and this route became known as the New Goodnight Trail.

Many trail drivers used a lead steer, which strode to the front of the herd and led the way. If a steer did its job well, it would not be sold but would come back from a trail drive to lead another. Charles Goodnight owned a lead steer named "Old Blue" that he'd bought from cattleman John Chisum. Goodnight put a bell around Old Blue's neck, and the other steers quickly learned to follow the familiar sound. The wrangler muffled the bell at night by stuffing it with grass or tying down the clapper with a strap. Old Blue, according to range legend, "could find the best water, the best grass, and the easiest river crossings," and he could even soothe a nervous herd during a storm with his reassuring bawl. Old Blue remained aloof from the herd at night, grazed with the saddle horses, and came into camp to beg snacks and biscuits from the cook. During eight seasons, more than ten thousand head of Goodnight cattle followed Old Blue to market, a one-way trip for them but not for Blue. He was never shipped to market, and after his last cattle drive, he retired to a permanent pasture on Goodnight's ranch and lived to be twenty years old. When Blue died, the cattleman mounted his horns in a place of honor in his ranch office.

In 1868, after several months moving herds up the Goodnight-Loving Trail, the cattleman returned to Fort Sumner and exhumed Loving's body. His cowboys gathered oil cans, beat them flat, and soldered them into a huge tin coffin and placed the original wooden one containing Loving's remains inside. Then they built a large wooden box to hold the metal coffin, packed several inches of powdered charcoal around it and sealed the lid. This was loaded into a wagon drawn by six mules and driven by Bose Ikard. On February 8, the funeral cortege, escorted by six of Loving's friends, left Fort Sumner and headed down the Goodnight-Loving Trail toward home in Weatherford, Texas. According to Loving's wishes, he was buried with Masonic honors at Greenwood Cemetery in Weatherford in March 1868. Years later, Oliver Loving was inducted into the National Cowboy Hall of Fame in Oklahoma City. Loving County, Texas, and Loving, New Mexico, were named in his honor.

In late December 1868, the *Colorado Chieftain* reported that Goodnight, "the well-known stock dealer, passed through Trinidad on his way back to Texas." The paper said that he planned to return with his family to make southern Colorado a permanent home. Loving's son Jim was with him, and the profits from cattle sales were concealed in a wagon driven by Bose Ikard. Goodnight kept his promise to Loving and gave his partner's family half of the $72,000 he'd earned after Loving's death, making them financially solvent.

Charles Goodnight continued to drive herds up the trail that bore his name for another nine years. Around 1869, he moved his headquarters to rolling land west of Pueblo, Colorado, where he built a house near the bluffs, naming it Rock Cañon Ranch. A large barn of hand-cut sandstone blocks housed the horses and livestock. Goodnight married in 1870, and he and his bride, Mary, settled into their new home. Three thousand longhorns grazed in lush, grassy meadows as far west as the Wet Mountains, and line camps were built to accommodate the cowboys. Goodnight dug ditches and irrigated fields of hay and corn and set out apple trees in the first orchards planted in southern Colorado. The cattleman was instrumental in founding the Stock Growers' Bank of Pueblo, a meatpacking company at Las Animas, and the Colorado Stock Raiser's Association in 1871. This progressive organization promoted branding of calves, recording brands, and fencing land to confine livestock.

The Financial Panic of 1873—brought about by the demonetization of silver, railroad speculation, and a severe drought—set off a worldwide depression that ruined many cattlemen. Goodnight lost much of his holdings, and in 1875, he moved his remaining cattle to northern New Mexico for

The Goodnight Barn near Pueblo, built of sandstone in 1870, is the sole surviving structure of Goodnight's Rock Cañon Ranch. *Goodnight Barn Preservation Committee.*

the winter. Then he returned to Texas and formed a partnership with John Adair, a Scottish investor he'd met in Denver. They started the JA Ranch in remote Palo Duro Canyon in the Texas Panhandle, and Goodnight drove his cattle to the new ranch. Eventually, the JA Ranch sprawled over more than 1 million acres and had more than 100,000 head of cattle. Goodnight developed the "cattalo" by crossing bison from his domestic buffalo herd with polled Angus cattle.

Black cowboys Frank Mayes, Jim Fowler, William Taylor, and Dan Sauls remained in Goodnight's crew for years and made several drives with the cattleman on the trail that bears his name. Dan Sauls had been a bronc buster in Oklahoma and the Panhandle before he joined the Goodnight-Loving crew. In the 1880s, he worked on drives from large Texas ranches moving cattle up the expanded Goodnight-Loving Trail to northeastern Colorado, Wyoming, and the grasslands in Montana. When Sauls grew older, he drove the water wagon on Goodnight's cattle drives.

Bose Ikard took part in every Goodnight trail drive to New Mexico and Colorado through 1869. Bose liked the Rocky Mountains and hoped to buy land near Goodnight's Pueblo ranch and start his own herd. When he told Goodnight about his idea, the cattleman advised against it because of the sparse population of Black workers in the Colorado Territory. Goodnight said that there "were so few Negroes in that country that he should stay in Texas and buy a farm." The census of 1860 recorded 46 Black people in Colorado, but ten years later, by 1870, there were 456. However, Bose took Goodnight's advice and gave up his dream, and after one last cattle drive, he remained behind in Weatherford. Bose joined his former owner, Milton Ikard, in a battle against Quanah Parker and his band of Comanches in 1869. He married, had six children, and worked as a handyman. He had many friends with whom he shared stories at cowboy reunions. Goodnight visited and sent him money occasionally.

When Bose was about eighty-five, he became ill with influenza and died on January 4, 1929. He was buried at Weatherford's Greenwood Cemetery near Oliver Loving's grave. Upon learning of his friend Bose's death, Goodnight had a granite monument designed for his grave and wrote an epitaph for his companion on the trail: "Served with me four years on the Goodnight-Loving Trail, never shirked a duty or disobeyed an order, rode with me in many stampedes, participated in three engagements with Comanches. Splendid behavior. C. Goodnight." When the monument was placed on Bose's grave in June 1929, the Weatherford newspaper of June 8 published Bose's complete obituary under the headline "Charles Goodnight

Bose Ikard, Black American cowboy and trusted friend of Charles Goodnight. He made several drives on the Goodnight-Loving Trail. *Public domain.*

Erects Monument to Negro Friend Buried Here" and included the epitaph written by Goodnight.

In his later years, Goodnight always spoke highly of Bose Ikard and praised his ability riding broncs, adding that he was "an exceptional night herder, and was also good with pans and skillets." In 1923, Goodnight was interviewed by J. Evetts Haley for his biography and said, "Bose surpassed any man I had in endurance and stamina. There was a dignity, a cleanliness, and a reliability about him that was wonderful. He paid no attention to women. His behavior was very good in a fight, and he was probably the most devoted man to me that I ever had. I have trusted him farther than any living man. He was my detective, banker, and everything else in Colorado, New Mexico, and the other wild country that I was in. The nearest and only bank was at Denver, and when we carried money, I gave it to Bose, for a thief would never think of robbing him—never think of looking in a Negro's bed for money." Goodnight recalled experiences with Bose, saying, "We went through some terrible trials during those four years on the trail. While I had a good constitution and endurance, after being in the saddle for several days and nights at a time, on various occasions, and finding I could stand it no longer, I would ask Bose if he would take my place, and he never failed to answer me in the most cheerful and willing manner, and was the most skilled and trustworthy man I had."

In just one season, Goodnight and Loving had blazed a trail that quickly gained prominence, and more than 600,000 cattle would soon move along it. In the spring of 1869, cattlemen Dudley and Snyder drove a herd of longhorns to Fort Sumner and sold their cattle to the army for thirty-six dollars per head. Another herd from Llano, Texas, took the southern portion of the Goodnight-Loving Trail to the Pecos, and after crossing the river, they continued along the old Butterfield stage route west to Tucson and Yuma. That same year, 2,500 head of cattle from Texas were successfully delivered to Los Angeles and sold for a profit. More longhorns went north on the

Goodnight-Loving Trail to Wyoming, where they supplied construction crews of the Union Pacific Railroad laying track across the plains.

In the late 1870s, Deer Trail, in eastern Colorado, became an important shipping point for livestock from southern Colorado and New Mexico. After the Atchison, Topeka, and Santa Fe competed a line through Trinidad, cattlemen began shipping their herds from that railhead.

Charles Goodnight died on December 12, 1926, and was buried at the Goodnight Cemetery on his ranch near Amarillo. He was one of the most respected and influential cattlemen of the West and was sometimes called the "Father of the Texas Panhandle." In 1955, Charles Goodnight was inducted into the Hall of Great Westerners of the National Cowboy & Western Heritage Museum.

PREPARING FOR A CATTLE DRIVE

Cattle drives usually began after spring roundup, when green grass was available along the trail and the herd could reach the railhead before cold weather. Cattle from several different ranches were often combined in one large herd, and the trail boss was responsible for keeping records of the number from each ranch, their brands, and earmarks. All the animals were marked with one trail brand to identify them if they became lost in a storm or stampede or fell behind on the trail.

A trail drive from Texas usually took several months to reach the shipping point in Kansas. While cattle could be driven as much as 25 miles in a single day, they would lose so much weight and would be in such poor condition that they would be hard to sell at the end of the trail. A good trail driver usually took the herd shorter distances, 10 to 15 miles each day, so the animals maintained a healthy weight. The drive stopped midday for water and to graze and rest before resuming the trail in the afternoon. Most trail bosses and the cook expected to stop for the night around 5:00 p.m. A 1,500-mile trail drive took four to six months, depending on the terrain, the conditions, and any unexpected events. An Indian attack, severe weather, or stampede could slow the herd's progress and delay the end of the drive.

A typical outfit consisted of an experienced trail boss and ten to twenty cowboys, each of whom had a string of five to ten horses. The trail boss was the final authority and was paid $100 to $125 per month. He contracted with ranchers to get their animals to market efficiently, with fewer cattle losses and hardships for the crew. He was familiar with the trails, water sources, and local tribes. Trail drivers were usually older and knew how to manage cattle and men. Experienced bosses were always in demand, and they hired experienced cowboys for their drives. In the 1880s and 1890s, some men worked only as trail bosses, contracting to deliver a herd to the railhead, negotiate a price, and sell the herd. The boss collected payment and deposited it in a bank or delivered the money to the owner. Some trail bosses had a small crew of cowboys and hired additional men locally. Professional trail drivers like Ab Blocker worked for the XIT Ranch and large cattle operations, taking big herds to market or moving them long distances. Ab had experienced crews, many of whom were Black, and he often took herds to New Mexico or Montana.

The cook drove the chuck wagon, was second in authority to the trail boss, and earned sixty to seventy-five dollars per month. The cook was often a veteran cowboy and was a respected member of the crew. He was in charge of the food supplies, the cowboys' bedrolls and possessions, and the medical supplies. Besides preparing the meals, he set the tone for the drive. Cowboy James Cook said, "A trail cook could do more towards making life pleasant for those about him than any other man in the outfit."

Most trail bosses hired twelve to eighteen cowboys to manage a herd of three thousand longhorns. Cowboys often left their ranch jobs temporarily

Cowboys sitting by supply wagons used on long cattle drives to carry grain for horses, tack, and supplies. *Library of Congress.*

to sign on to a cattle drive from another ranch. When the herd reached the railhead, cowboys were paid and returned to their ranch jobs. Some cowboys worked steadily on cattle drives most of the year, delivering herds to shipping points in Kansas or to new ranchers in New Mexico and Colorado. The trail boss hired his crew of cowboys carefully, selecting only the most skilled and dependable. They were usually young, mere boys to men in their early twenties, but their youthful appearance often belied their experience. Most of the time, greenhorns were left at home unless they were hired as wranglers.

There were at least four Black cowboys on almost every cattle drive. They handled the same jobs as the white cowboys and were paid equal wages, about thirty dollars per month. Black cowboys ate the same food, slept on the ground, walked the same streets, and faced the same challenges and difficulties as the white men. George Saunders of the Texas Trail Drivers Association, a well-respected authority on the history of trail drives, estimated that of the thirty-five thousand men who "went up the trail" from Texas with herds between 1865 to 1895, "about one-third were Negroes and Mexicans." This estimate is verified by the existing lists of outfits that identified their members by race. These old lists show that Blacks outnumbered Mexicans by more than two to one. On the drives, 63 percent of the men were white, 25 percent were Black, and slightly less than 12 percent were Mexican. A typical trail drive with twelve cowboys had seven or eight white cowboys, including the trail boss, and three Black cowboys, one of whom might be the cook and another might be the wrangler, while the third was a trail hand. On this typical drive, there were usually one or two Mexicans. Sometimes as many as 40 percent of the cowboys on a drive were Black. One trail drive in 1874 had a crew with a white trail boss, while all the cowboys were Black.

A boss said, "A cowboy needed steady nerves, deft hands, and firm muscles, and he should be able to endure hardship and stay alert for sudden danger. He must be able to ride well, work from a horse, take care of horses, understand and be able to live with a horse. He should be skilled at roping cattle and know how to shoot a rifle and six-shooter accurately. An understanding of the nature of longhorns and their instincts was expected."

E.C. "Teddy Blue" Abbott left home when he was about fourteen to become a cowboy and ride the range during the 1870s and 1880s. His stories paint a colorful picture of cowboy life in *We Pointed Them North*, first published in 1939. Teddy said, "Other old-timers have told all about stampedes and swimming rivers and what a terrible time we had, but they never put in any of the fun, and fun was at least half of it." Teddy described most trail driving cowboys as young and quick, of wiry build, middle-sized, and hard on horses. He commented that cowboys were "good natured" and endured the hardships of the trail without complaint. Teddy said, "It didn't pay to be anything else. I have seen them ride into camp after two days and two nights on herd, lay down on their saddle blankets in the rain and sleep like dead men, then get up laughing and joking about some good time they had in Ogallala or Dodge City." Most of the young cowboys thought that enduring sixteen hours in the saddle, breathing dense clouds of choking dust, was worth the adventures and a rambunctious celebration at the end of the trail. Trail bosses liked to hire some older, trusted cowboys for their experience and the calming effect they had on the younger, wilder men. Mature Black cowboys like Ben Kinchlow, who'd been breaking horses and driving cattle since he was fourteen, were needed in trail crews. They were likely to return year after year, unlike many white cowboys, who quickly tired of the dust and exhausting grind.

The wrangler was responsible for the horse herd, called the "remuda," and he was the cook's helper. He was often very young, with little or no experience, and was paid less than the cowboys. The wrangler herded a remuda that was as small as twenty horses or one with more than one hundred animals. He had to see that the horses were fed, watered, and secured at night, safe from roaming Indians. If he didn't handle his job well, the cowboys couldn't do theirs. Tenderfeet, farm boys, former gamblers, soldiers, or freighters started up the trail the first time as wranglers in hopes of becoming cowboys. Young Black youths, drawn by the freedom of a cowboy's life, eagerly signed on to wrangle the horses, a job many had already handled at home. One of the youngest wranglers on a John Chisum drive was an eight-year-old Black boy.

Cowboys were paid thirty to forty dollars per month. Experience counted, and some who'd spent a great deal of time on the trail earned sixty dollars instead of the usual thirty. This was kept quiet, although everyone knew that the cook earned more than a cowhand. By the 1890s, wages had generally increased but still varied depending on the area. The cowboys on the northern ranges of Montana, Wyoming, and Dakota Territory earned more than those in Kansas and Texas.

The cowboy's distinctive working gear, most of it derived from the Mexican *vaquero*, captured the public's imagination. The high-crowned felt hat with its wide brim protected his face from the sun and rain. Boots with two-inch heels kept his feet in the stirrups and improved his balance and stability while riding. The bandanna around his neck could be pulled up over his nose to protect against dust, howling wind, and stinging sleet.

Right: Ben Kinchlow, former slave who became a cowboy. *Library of Congress.*

Below: Black cowboys standing beside a horse, early 1900s. *University of Texas–San Antonio Libraries Special Collections.*

Chaps of cowhide, sheepskin, goatskin, bear, or buffalo were worn to protect against scratches from thick brush, cactus, and thorns and added warmth in cold weather. Spurs, sometimes called "grappling irons," were nickel plated or silver and were worn to communicate with the horse. A cowboy's saddle often cost more than his horse, and since he might spend twenty hours sitting in it, it had to be comfortable and sturdy. The saddle went with him from job to job. Cowboys were often bowlegged from spending so much time on horseback, and they usually had long hair. There were no barbers on trail drives, and there was no time for a haircut. Because weight was important, cowboys were allowed to take only a few blankets and some extra clothing on a drive. Everything was stuffed in a sack and piled on the chuck wagon.

The cowboy's best friend was his horse, and the animal was his most understanding work partner. The horse was indispensable transportation, and a cowboy's safety, even his life, could depend on his horse. Every cowboy was given a number of horses to ride as long as he was on the job. The horses were used for different tasks: saddle horses were ridden a few hours daily on the trail, while a night horse was used to ride guard around the herd at night. The saddle horses were usually smaller mustangs or quarter horses, strong and tough, able to endure being ridden for miles day after day. A good night horse was invaluable and prized along with cutting and roping horses. A night horse needed good eyesight and intelligence and must be surefooted to reduce the danger of falling while he was running with a stampede. This horse had to be able to find his way back to camp even on the darkest night after running miles. Jesse Benton, a longtime cowboy, said, "In a stampede, it made no difference how far from camp you were or how dark the night, he would get you back. Many a tired cowboy after a stampede was six or seven miles from camp with the night dark as coal…just give that horse his head and he would take you straight back to camp." The night horse had common sense and was often a cowboy's most intelligent horse. Roping and cutting horses had specialized training and were used more often at the home ranch. In the early years of the large cattle drives, cowboys who were returning to their ranch job rode their horse back. After railroads reached a wide area, once the cattle were loaded in stock cars, the trail boss sold most of the horses, and the cowboys rode the train back to the ranch.

LONG DAYS ON THE TRAIL

The cowboy's day began before dawn to the sounds of the cook banging his pots and kettles and the aroma of strong coffee drifting on the cold morning air. When the cook yelled, "Come an' git it!" everyone lined up for breakfast as the last two men on night guard came in. The wrangler brought the horses into camp, and after each cowboy had eaten and stacked his dishes in the pan, he caught his mount for the morning. There was the usual commotion as some horses limbered up with a few corkscrew bucks and crow hops before settling down. One of the Black cowboys, usually Ad Jones or Jim Perry if they were in the crew, would climb into the saddle and take the kinks out of those broncs quickly.

Once the dishes were washed, the wrangler helped the cook load the chuck wagon. Then he hitched up the team and got the remuda ready to go. The cook climbed onto the chuck wagon seat, released the brake, clucked to the team, and swung the wagon onto the trail ahead of the herd. The wrangler drove the remuda into position near the side of the chuck wagon.

The cattle were awake and grazing quietly, and the lead steer was waiting in his place when the trail boss gave the signal to start by waving his hat forward. This signaled the point men to start the herd moving, and the cattle fell into place behind the lead steer. The cowboys riding point and the swing men repeated the forward motion with their hats, and the signal was passed back along the herd to the drag men. The lead steer's even stride kept the herd moving forward at a regular rate. As the cattle plodded along at a leisurely pace, each one kept relatively the same position in line, and cattle were soon strung out in a column fifty or sixty feet wide and about a mile long.

Cowboys were assigned their positions around the herd by the trail boss. The point or lead rider near the front of the herd determined the direction, controlled the speed, and gave the cattle something to follow. Larger herds sometimes used two point men. An honored position on the drive, this job was reserved for more experienced hands who knew the country and the trail. The strongest, most restless steers that were more likely to try to break away were at the front of herd.

Swing riders rode closely along each side of the herd, about a third of the way back from the point rider. They kept the cattle together and were on the lookout for animals that tried to leave the herd. If the point man left his position, a swing rider moved into his place until he returned.

The flank rider was two-thirds of the way back, where the cattle were less troublesome. He backed up the swing riders and kept the cattle bunched together, preventing the back of the herd from fanning out along the trail.

The drag riders were in the rear, keeping the herd moving and pushing the slower animals along. Tired, injured animals were here, and this unpleasant spot in the choking dust was usually reserved for inexperienced cowboys. Some trail bosses rotated riders through all the positions except point, but for many drives, the position you were assigned remained yours for the drive. The trail boss rode ahead of the herd to check the trail and watch for obstacles, Indians, and rustlers.

Cowboys watched the cattle closely. The first few days, when the herd was being "road broke," were crucial as the cattle grew accustomed to the trail and the routine. If they could be kept from stampeding the first ten days, they'd be much easier to handle the rest of the drive. Some trail bosses pushed the cattle hard at first so they'd be tired and less restless at night. Other bosses coddled the animals along on short, easy drives so they'd stay calm and be eager to rest at night.

If he was taking the herd over an unfamiliar route, the boss was up early in the morning looking for a good spot with grass for the herd's noontime rest. At about 11:00 a.m., he'd signal the point men to stop, and the cattle were allowed to graze along the trail as the cowboys headed for the chuck wagon. The wrangler brought in fresh horses, returning tired animals to the remuda. When the cattle began lying down, the trail boss knew that they'd grazed enough and signaled the cowboys to get them moving again.

A good trail boss got the herd to market as quickly as possible but delivered cattle that were in good condition with a healthy weight. If they traveled

Cowboy on horseback herding Kohrs cattle in Eastern Montana, circa 1910. *Grant-Kohrs Ranch National Historic Site.*

about fifteen miles each day and were allowed to rest and graze at midday, cattle maintained a healthy weight, requiring about two to three months to travel from the home ranch to the railhead.

In the afternoon, the trail boss rode ahead to find a good spot for the evening camp and a bedding ground for the cattle near a stream or watering hole with grass for grazing. Timbered areas where Indians and predators could hide were avoided, as well as ravines that stampeding cattle could fall into. The cook drove ahead with the wrangler and the remuda to arrive at the bedding ground before the herd. He got the cook fire going and the evening meal started, while the wrangler hobbled the horses and collected more fuel for the fire.

The afternoon drive was easier, as the cattle were tired and thirsty. Cowboys liked to arrive at the bedding ground before sundown so there was time to water the herd and get the cattle settled for the night. The herd was divided into bunches to decrease crowding and pushing at the river or water hole. A longhorn could drink up to thirty gallons of water a day, and without plenty of fresh water, cattle became irritable and would stampede. While the cowboys were watering the herd and getting them bedded down for the night, the cook was at work. Dinner was the highlight of the cowboys' day, and if there was time, the cook might even make a dessert for the boys.

Before nightfall, the wrangler brought in the night horses, hobbled them, and put them in a rope corral, where they stayed until the cowboys needed them for their guard shifts. The longhorns were slowly pushed into a circle on a large grassy area where they weren't crowded together and could graze or lie down. They had a big appetite in the evening, and as darkness fell, they chewed their cud and yawned. As the whippoorwills called, the tired cattle sank to their knees, and when they were bedded down, all the hands except two on guard rode back to camp.

The weary cowboys gathered around the campfire for supper and then got their blanket rolls from the chuck wagon. The blankets and a couple of quilts, called "soogans," were rolled up in a tarp and secured with a rope at each end to keep them dry. The tarp was spread on the ground, topped with the blankets and soogans. Most cowboys slept in their clothes unless it was hot, and then they'd strip down to their underwear. Boots and belts were usually taken off unless they were afraid of an Indian attack. There might be a bit of talk or a little music, but weariness usually prevailed and they quickly fell asleep. If it rained or snowed, a cowboy covered his head with the tarp, pulled up the sides and tucked them in tightly around his body to keep out the moisture.

In cold weather, cowboys sometimes put their beds together to share body heat and keep warm. When there were frequent Indian raids or the cattle were restless and stampeding often, a cowboy might not take his boots off for a week. When a long rainy spell made the ground boggy and the cattle irritable, cowhands got little sleep. Often three riders would spread their beds on the ground in a triangle and lie down with each man using his neighbor's ankles as a pillow, keeping his head out of the mire. When the cattle were

Cowboys, *vaqueros*, and bronco busters, Denver, Colorado, circa 1905. Bill Pickett is farthest to left in photo. *Solomon Butcher, Nebraska State Historical Society.*

restless or there was an Indian threat, every cowboy kept his horse close by, holding on to the bridle reins as he dozed. Cowboys on the trail were always short on sleep, so they valued any horizontal time they got.

The cook kept a pot of hot coffee on the fire all night. Cowboys going on night guard grabbed a cup of the strong brew to keep awake, and men coming in from a cold night ride appreciated the warmth of a hot cup. Night guard duty was usually divided into two-hour shifts, with two men to each shift. They rode around the herd, each going in opposite directions, turning back any stragglers that got up during the night and tried to leave. Jesse Benton, a cowboy who wrote about his trail driving days in *Cow by the Tail*, said, "Each steer needed about 100 square feet to keep him comfortable with his big horns. It took quite a piece of ground to bed down 2000 steers, and you can figure how many times a cowboy would ride around that herd at night." Benton continued, "To ride around the big steers by nightfall, lying down full as ticks, chewing their cuds and blowing, with the moon shining on their big horns was a sight to make a man's eyes pop."

About midnight, the longhorns would get up, graze a bit and then lie down, only to get up again. Some grazed off and on all night. Black cowboy John Sneed said, "We always had some steers that wouldn't bed down at all. They'd go ten to thirty feet away, and we'd let them alone." During the night, cowboys hummed and sang to the cattle to soothe them and keep them calm, reducing the chance of stampedes. Lonesome songs could be heard drifting on the breeze, while the big night sky was full of stars, shining like candles.

It wasn't unusual for a tired cowboy riding night guard to nod off to sleep while still keeping his seat in the saddle. His night horse would continue to jog around the herd without a touch of the reins, pushing back every cow that that tried to escape. Cowboy Jim Olson said his night horse could tell you within fifteen minutes when his shift was almost over, and it was time to go and wake up the next cowboy on night guard. Other cowboys agreed that their night horse always knew within a few minutes when it was time to stop circling the cattle and return to camp. Some said their animal might start shaking his head or pulling on the bit, and they depended on their horse to keep track of the time.

When his guard shift ended, the cowboy rode into camp and woke his relief by talking to him. He didn't touch or shake him because a startled man was liable to grab his six-shooter. When the morning star came up, the cattle grew restless and got up because they didn't need an alarm clock to signal the start of a new day.

Cowboy Charlie Willis had a soothing voice that calmed restless longhorns when he sang to them. Born enslaved in 1847, by the time he was twenty-four, Charlie had ridden thousands of miles on the Goodnight-Loving and Chisolm Trails. When he wasn't on cattle drives, he broke and trained mustangs at the Morris ranch near Bartlett, Texas. Charlie was known for the songs he brought back from the trail, and sometimes he put together his own ballads. Around 1871, he returned from a cattle drive singing a new song that he called "Good-Bye, Old Paint." He taught it to Morris's seven-year-old son, Jesse, who learned to play it on his fiddle.

The song became part of the trail driving cowboys' repertoire of midnight ballads crooned to the longhorns. It was eventually heard by Jack Thorp, a New Mexico cowboy, who in 1889 began writing down songs he heard around the campfire. In 1908, he published a little booklet, *Songs of the Cowboy*, containing twenty-four songs. Thorp was the first person to collect and preserve these ballads of the West, and in 1921, Houghton Mifflin published his larger collection of more than one hundred cowboy songs.

Years later, in 1942, a pioneering musicologist and folklorist, John Lomax, recorded Jesse Morris, now an adult and a talented fiddler, singing and playing Charlie Willis's song "Good-Bye, Old Paint." Lomax sent the recording to the American Folklife Center at the Library of Congress, where it is preserved today. Charlie worked at the Morris Ranch for more than twenty years, married, and raised seven children. He died at eighty and was

Photo postcard of a Black cowboy from the early 1900s. *Collection of the Smithsonian National Museum of African American History and Culture.*

buried in 1930 near his home. There are hundreds of ballads and songs that were made up by cowboys and sung to pass the time on the trail or while riding night herd. The composers of historic classics like "Git Along Little Doggies," "Strawberry Roan," "Red River Valley," "Oh, Bury Me Not on the Lone Prairie," and hundreds more are unknown. Charlie Willis is credited with composing "Good-Bye, Old Paint."

DANGERS OF THE CATTLE DRIVE

Driving cattle to market presented many challenges, and it could be dangerous. There were miles of open prairie; barren, waterless plains and dry deserts; and rivers full of quicksand. There were fierce winds, unexpected blizzards, thunderstorms, and dangerous lightning, which stampeded herds and scattered cattle. Comanches and Kiowas roamed the plains, and Apaches lurked in the rugged territory west of the Pecos, while rustlers stampeded and drove off cattle. The cowboys put in long hours and endured the monotony of routine, fatigue from long hours in the saddle, and the misery of exposure to the elements. They worked in freezing cold or blistering sun and in ice, snow, and heavy rain.

Lonely graves along the trail were sobering reminders of the dangers—their markers said simply "Killed by Indians," "Died in Stampede," or "Hit by Lightning." There were more at river crossings: "Drowned," "Died crossin' river," "Snake bit." Sudden illness, appendicitis, pneumonia, blood poisoning, a snakebite, a throw from a horse, or dragged when a boot caught in a stirrup were all misfortunes that could bring death.

During the 1860s, large numbers of Indians roamed Texas, Kansas, eastern New Mexico, and Colorado. The early cattle drives were often attacked by raiding parties that stampeded and ran off cattle. Indians demanded beef to allow a herd to pass through their territory, and sometimes they blocked herds and kept them from moving on, while the braves killed steers at random. These losses varied from forty or fifty head of cattle to sometimes

The only known photograph of the Rufus Buck Gang, taken in the summer of 1895 in Indian Territory. Buck is in the middle. *Public domain.*

losing the entire herd. Often the real goal of the Indians was to steal the horses. If a wrangler was guarding the remuda alone, he had little chance of keeping the horses against a war party. If the Indians succeeded in grabbing the remuda, the cowboys who were left on foot with a herd of longhorns to get to market were in a predicament.

After Comanche leader Quanah Parker surrendered in 1875 and took his followers to a reservation, the attacks decreased, but Indians continued to demand cattle and steal horses. There was little law enforcement on the plains or in Indian Territory, so trail drivers had to depend on their own resources. Trail bosses who were traveling near other herds on the trail sometimes banded together to fight off rustlers or Indians. Farmers, fearing Texas Fever, occasionally stampeded the longhorns passing through their region to prevent them from exposing their domestic cattle.

Treacherous river crossings were responsible for as many cattle losses as Indians and rustlers combined. The trail boss hoped that the high water from spring snowmelt had subsided by the time his herd reached a river. He had to locate a spot for the herd to cross that had firm footing on each bank and avoided high sandbars of quicksand. Sometimes the cattle were divided into bunches of thirty and urged into the water, following the lead steer or a mounted cowboy. As the cattle moved into the water, mounted cowboys rode along both sides and the rear of the herd to keep them moving forward.

Any river crossing could be bad luck for a cowboy who couldn't swim. When crossing, if the cattle were startled by a whirlpool, a floating tree, or a strange sound, they might start milling around in a circle and could be swept downstream and drowned. To stop this milling, cowboys rode directly into the swirling mass, yelling and swatting the animals, turning them toward the riverbank. Sometimes a cowboy was knocked off his horse into the water and the dangerous crush of sharp horns and flailing hooves. Swimming in the midst of this would be nearly impossible, so he'd have to act quickly and grab the tail of a steer or horse and be towed to the bank.

Cattle often balked at going into the water until the lead steer stepped in boldly, and then they usually fell in line behind him. Ab Blocker, a trail driver who moved thousands of cattle north for the XIT Ranch, often used a pair of oxen to pull the chuck wagon. One animal named "Bully" was described as "highly individualized" because of his unusual attachment to the chuck wagon. When he wasn't pulling it, he followed the wagon as closely as possible, refusing to leave it even to rest. When Ab's cattle drive reached the Platte River in Colorado, the water was high, full of ice, and very cold from melting snow. The cattle balked at crossing, but Frank, a Black cowboy, had a suggestion. Instead of forcing the longhorns into the frigid water, the herd could go up river a few miles to an old army bridge. Since cattle often needed urging to cross a bridge, the chuck wagon would start across first, while Bully and the lead steer were held back. When the chuck wagon was halfway across, Bully would be let loose, and as he bolted onto the bridge, hopefully, the lead steer and the rest of the herd would

Cowboys crossing a river. *Grant-Kohrs National Historic Site.*

follow him. Blocker tried it, Bully dashed across the bridge, and the entire herd thundered after him. Later, Ab recalled, "That great herd of cattle was strung out across the bridge like a remuda of horses—the first bridge any steer had ever put a foot upon."

Quicksand often wasn't seen until the cattle started across the river and became bogged down in it. The treacherous sand closed around the animal's legs, and if it wasn't rescued quickly, it often drowned. Extracting a terrified longhorn was hard work and dangerous. One man roped the trapped animal, tied the rope to his saddle horn, and used his horse to pull the longhorn out, while another man grabbed the tail and pulled. If they got the longhorn out of the quicksand, they stood it on its feet, avoiding the horns, hoping it would stagger off. Some longhorns recovered quickly, charged their rescuers and everything in sight, and were a danger to horses, mules, cowboys, even the chuck wagon.

Cattle drives usually had to cross several rivers, and when the water was low, the cook drove the chuck wagon across without problems. Swiftly moving high water was a challenge, and the trail boss might wait a few days for the water level to drop. Everyone was anxious to get the chuck wagon and food supplies safely across the river or nobody would eat. Sometimes trees were cut down, and logs about sixteen feet long were tied on both sides of the chuck wagon. Then the team was hitched up and started across with the floating wagon. Sometimes six to eight mounted cowboys would tow the chuck wagon across the river.

Good clean water for the cowboys and cattle to drink was never taken for granted. Water in rivers could be full of mud, silt, the carcasses of dead animals, and animal waste. The water in the Pecos and many rivers running through deserts was alkaline, and cowboys on the Goodnight-Loving Trail were often confronted with bad water. This tasted terrible and could cause diarrhea. Experienced outfits traveling the Goodnight-Loving Trail carried crates of canned tomatoes so the cowboys could drink the thirst-quenching juice instead of bad Pecos River water. Some crews carried ginger to offset the bad water, while others mixed soda and vinegar with water, making an effervescent concoction that they quickly gulped down.

During the 1880s, there was a drought in Texas and New Mexico, and the grass and streams near the Goodnight-Loving Trail dried up. Herds walked off much of their weight and were so weak when they reached the Pecos that they tumbled down the steep banks. Then they drank so much of the alkaline water that they lay down and died. Others, with their bellies weighted down by the bad water, tottered along on weak legs, right into the grasping quicksands of the Pecos. They bogged down and died without moving far from the edge of the river.

Black cowboy Frank Chisum was working on a roundup in 1886 near John Chisum's Roswell, New Mexico ranch during a severe drought. The water holes and small lakes that watered Chisum's huge herds were drying up. Thirsty cattle died in bunches in the mud, and when the rains finally came, their carcasses rotted, polluting the water. When Frank started to get a drink from a water hole, Dick, the Black cook, stopped him, warning that the water had to be strained first to remove the maggots! The Pecos River was also full of screwworms from cattle carcasses, and everyone who had to use this water strained it first through a gunnysack. During this drought, the cattle loss was staggering, and piles of carcasses lined the banks of the Pecos for miles.

A cowboy slept on the ground, rolled up in his blankets with his saddle as a pillow. He never knew if he'd wake up to find a rattlesnake cuddled up next to him for warmth or if a snake might strike his horse's leg or nose while riding on the trail. A snakebite could be serious or fatal for both man and horse and often caused terrible, necrotic wounds that took forever to heal. Rattlesnakes spooked horses and often bit wranglers who spent most of their time on foot. One Black wrangler named Dick, who was bitten on his thumb, hurried to the chuck wagon, sucking on the bite to extract the venom. His hand and arm were already swollen and inflamed. Another cowboy immediately drew his knife and cut an *X* gash around the fang marks, and then he opened a pistol cartridge, poured gunpowder into the wound, and lit it with a match. Surprisingly, Dick survived the snakebite and the first-aid treatment!

The cook could dispense home remedies and laxatives for everything from bellyaches, bruises, and boils to broken bones, and occasionally he had to pull a bad tooth or sew up a jagged cut. If a cowboy was seriously injured in a fall from a half-broken horse or wounded by an Indian arrow, there wasn't a lot the cook could do. A simple cut could become infected and bring raging fever and gangrene. Lack of sleep and nights lying on the cold, damp ground under thin, worn blankets could lead to suffocating pneumonia. If a cowboy was soaked in a storm and developed pneumonia or a lung infection from swimming cattle across rivers, a quick recovery or a lingering death was the usual outcome. A sudden attack of appendicitis could be fatal. Cowboys exhausted by overwork, sixteen-hour days in the saddle, and lack of sleep were susceptible to smallpox, cholera, and other diseases. Rabid coyotes could infect cattle dogs. If the injury or ailment was serious, there was usually no medical help for miles around. All the cook could do was comfort his patient and hear his last wishes. If a town was nearby, the doctor would be sent for, or the patient would be loaded into a wagon and taken to him. No cowboy wanted to leave a companion in a lonely grave by the side of the trail.

In the spring of 1870, thirty-six-year-old cattleman Robert Johnson drove a herd of longhorns to Abilene, where he became ill and suddenly died. George Glenn, a young Black cowboy in his crew, took charge of having the rancher embalmed and buried in a metal casket at the Abilene cemetery. Glenn had been born into slavery in Colorado County, Texas, in 1850 and grew up on Johnson's ranch. Like many slaves, he'd taken care of cattle since he was a boy, and after emancipation, he had continued working for Johnson, becoming his trusted top hand.

The following year, in September 1871, Glenn returned to Abilene and had Johnson's casket disinterred and packed carefully in a wagon. Then he drove the wagon for forty-two days across three states to take Johnson's body back to Texas. When he reached Columbus, Texas, Glenn arranged a proper funeral and the burial of Johnson in the cemetery.

Little is known about George Glenn's life after Johnson died, but he probably continued working at local ranches. At the annual meetings of the Trail Drivers Association in 1924 and 1926, Glenn was honored as one of the few Black members of this organization, which preserves the memory of the old trail drivers. Glenn died of pneumonia in 1931 and is buried at Columbus, Texas.

Cattle drives that hit the trail when the grass was turning green could be surprised by a late spring snowstorm, which brought cold weather that was hard on the cowboys and their horses. Ab Blocker told of a drive to Dodge City when the weather was "fiercely cold," and the cattle stampeded every night. One morning, a cold northwest wind and a driving rain sent the herd running in all directions again. The cowboys rode for hours and finally managed to get the cattle rounded up before nightfall. Blocker said, "When we unsaddled that evening, our horses were tired and wet with sweat; the next morning we found every one of 'em stretched out dead, simply chilled to death."

During the summer, the trail boss's goal was to get the herd to the railroad before the first snow fell. "Negro Hal" remembered a sudden, late summer snowstorm when he was on a drive with the XIT Ranch in Texas. The trail boss told the cowboys to dig a hole in the sand that was ten feet

Bill Pickett and another Black cowboy at National Western Stock Show Rodeo in Denver, circa 1905. *Solomon Butcher, Nebraska State Historical Society.*

deep and large enough for all of them to get into. He said, "We even had a small fire in the middle to keep warm." The next morning, when Hal and the others emerged from their dugout, snowdrifts covered everything, and a fierce wind was blowing; however, the sun was shining and they pushed on.

John Young, a rugged old cowboy, recounted some of his experiences to J. Frank Dobie in *A Vaquero of the Brush Country*. On one cattle drive, he said, "We had a Negro cowboy called George, who was not very well clad because he liked to pike at monte too well to buy clothes." There had been a lot of bad weather, and most of the cowboys had colds and terrible coughs and sounded, "like a bunch of pot hounds baying a possum when we tried to sleep." Young said that on one bitter cold night, when he was riding night herd with George, the Black cowboy seemed really sick. "I tried to get him to go to the chuck wagon and turn his horse loose, but he was too game for that. His teeth were chattering, and he said to me, 'I can stand it if the rest of you all can.' Presently I saw him lean over his saddle horn coughing, and he looked like he was losing his breath. By the time I got to him, he was off his horse as dead as a mackerel and as stiff as a poker. He had simply frozen to death sitting on that horse! We placed his body in the chuckwagon on his bed and drove to the Palo Duro. On the highest hill that we could find, we planted that poor Black boy, rolled in his blankets." He went on, "The ground was sandy so we could dig a grave deep enough so the coyotes would not claw into it."

Bill "Tige" Avery had some miserable experiences in Colorado blizzards, and he always kept a close eye on the weather and often volunteered to go ahead of the others to start a fire so they "could warm up." Tige was born enslaved around 1853 in Texas and grew up with the owner's son, John "Bud" Matthews. When they were both about nineteen years old, Bud Matthews and Tige began driving cattle over the Goodnight-Loving Trail to New Mexico and Colorado, up the Chisholm Trail to Kansas and later on the Great Western Trail to Montana and the Dakota Territory. In the 1870s, the Mattews family became partners with the Reynolds brothers in the cattle business.

In 1881, Tige was with a Reynolds trail crew driving a herd to the Indian agencies in Montana when a late spring blizzard hit. The weather was frigid, and when the temperature dropped below zero, Reynolds told the cowboys to let the cattle drift and take shelter in the chuck wagon. They rolled up in their blankets, trying to avoid freezing, but Tige wrapped his blankets around the shivering Reynolds and kept only his coat for warmth.

Reynolds would have none of that and insisted the cowboy share the blankets with him. The drifts piled up, but despite the frigid temperature and howling winds, Tige, Reynolds, and the crew survived; nonetheless, they lost every horse, frozen to death.

In 1891, Tige was with another trail crew, led by Phin Reynolds, driving four thousand head of cattle from the Panhandle through Colorado on the Goodnight-Loving Trail. On June 1, a devastating snowstorm struck them north of Hugo, Colorado, with fierce winds that whipped the blinding snow into deep drifts, blocking the trail. The frightened cattle scattered, mixing with other herds that were also on the trail, and soon more than fifteen thousand longhorns were drifting south ahead of the blizzard.

The temperature was below zero, and some cowboys' hands and feet showed signs of frostbite. Phin, Tige, and the others piled into the chuck wagon and crowded together under tarpaulins, blankets, and piles of clothing, trying to keep warm in the dangerously cold weather. When the wind finally died down and the snow faded away, they cautiously emerged from their shelter. Huge drifts completely covered the chuck wagon, and the deep snow made walking nearly impossible. All the cowboys survived, but the horses had no protection from the storm, and every animal perished. It took Phin's crew and numerous cowboys from other outfits six days to round up all the scattered cattle. They had drifted south twenty-five miles, and they only stopped when they ran up against the Union Pacific drift fences along the tracks. Hundreds of cattle froze, huddled along that fence.

Tige could neither read nor write, but he had a sharp mind, a quick wit, and great sense of humor. He rode broncs and was an outstanding roper, despite his hand that was disabled by a severe rope burn. Tige worked for the Matthews-Reynolds Ranch his entire life and taught their children and grandchildren the finer points of cowboying. Bud Matthews always praised his ability, saying, "Tige was what a good cowboy should be." Walt Matthews, Bud's son, credited Tige for "making me the cowboy I am today."

Tige Avery never married, and around 1930, he moved to town. Every morning, Bud, his lifelong friend, picked him up and took him to breakfast at the ranch. Tige never missed the annual Texas Cowboy Reunion, but in 1935, he became ill while at the celebration. He was hospitalized, but he died shortly after. Walt Matthews conducted Tige's funeral service, reminiscing about his teacher's trail experiences and the many kindnesses he'd done for others. Tige Avery was buried on the Matthews ranch, where he had spent all of his life. Bud Matthews, his old friend and employer, died a few years later in 1941.

Ab Blocker often worked with the same crew of cowboys on the long drives from the XIT Ranch in Texas to Montana. Many cowboys were Black—there was Bob Leavitt; Frank, who was known as "Ab's roper"; "Big Gus"; Newt Glendennon; Joe Tasby; and a cowboy known only as "Charlie." Jim Perry, an all-around top hand for the XIT, usually cooked on these long drives, although Bob Leavitt sometimes handled the job.

STAMPEDE!

There were plenty of dangers on the trail, but the most dreaded was a stampede. Every cowboy who ever trailed a herd worried about it whenever longhorn cattle were "jumpy and skittish." They were more likely to stampede than domesticated cattle, and anything could start them running. A cowboy would be riding around a herd under the moon and stars while the cattle were lying down contentedly chewing their cud. Then suddenly, the animals would bound to their feet and take off like the wind.

It didn't take much to make longhorns stampede: a sudden noise, the clatter of a dropped pot, a coyote's howl, a cowhand's sneeze, the flare of a match, a horse's sudden snort, the hiss of a rattlesnake, and more. Storms with sheets of blinding rain or sudden hail could set the herd off, and even a snapped twig could start the cattle's senseless running. In an instant, the herd became a solid mass of hooves and horns as thousands of cattle raced headlong in mad panic. Cowboys knew that thirsty cattle stampeded easily, and this was a constant danger on a drive if there wasn't enough water along the trail. Indians started stampedes by burning a sack of buffalo hair on the windward side of a herd. While the cowboys were chasing the cattle, the Indians would steal their horses and gather a few stray longhorns for their trouble.

Besides the danger to cowboys and their horses in a stampede, the cattle themselves were at great risk. In Idaho, an 1889 stampede led to the deaths of one cowboy and 341 longhorns. In Nebraska in 1876, four cowboys

"Stamped Herd." *J.A. Castaigne, from* Scribner's Magazine.

tried to head off 500 stampeding steers. Three of the men survived, but all that was left of the fourth was the handle of his revolver. The scent of a panther (mountain lion) prowling around the chuck wagon started a stampede in New Mexico, and another large herd began running when a tobacco shred from a cowboy's pouch blew into a steer's eye. That unfortunate crew lost two cowboys, a score more were injured, and 400 cattle were killed. One of the worst stampedes occurred in July 1876, near the Brazos River in Texas, when a herd of 15,000 cattle stampeded in an electrical storm and couldn't be turned back from a steep-sided gully. The crazed animals rushed off the edge, piling on top of one another, filling the ravine with 2,700 bellowing, dying steers.

Cowboys tried to avoid a stampede by keeping the herd calm, and they were especially alert when a storm was on the horizon. There was a sinister stillness in the air as ominous, dark clouds loomed overhead, their wispy tendrils touching the ground. Cattle rose to their feet and began moving around, bawling as the faint, far-off rumble of thunder and distant flashes of lightning slowly came closer. As a cowboy crooned a ballad to quiet the restless herd, more cattle got to their feet, milling about, tossing their heads, and rattling their horns.

The air crackled with electricity, and as clouds obscured the moon, the only light came from little balls of fire boiling around the tips of the cattle's horns. Halos of light flickered around their heads, and even their eyes seemed to be on fire. Tiny flickers of flames outlined the horses' ears and darted through their manes, while sparks danced across a cowboy's mustache.

Then a sudden flash of lightning cast a blinding, bluish light over the herd, giving it a ghostly, foreboding appearance. A sudden, deafening clap of thunder started the herd running; the ground shook as the terrified beasts raced blindly forward, and the pounding of their hooves could be heard above the storm. The crazed animals could knock down a tree whose trunk was as big as a man, or it might split and run around an obstacle and come together again. A herd would race headlong through a camp, knock over the chuck wagon, smash it flat, and then break apart into bunches heading in different directions. A stampede is a fearsome sight that cowboy Nat Love once described as a "maddening, plunging, snorting, bellowing mass of horns and hoofs!" This seething mass of cattle gives off an intense heat so hot that "a cowboy's face could be blistered as if he'd been struck by a blast from a furnace," warned Charles Goodnight.

Stampedes occurred more often at night, when darkness hid the dangers of prairie dog holes that could trip a horse, the crumbling edges of cliffs and ravines, unseen boulders, rocks, trees, and slick, slippery spots of ground. These shadowy hazards could turn even the best mount into a stumbling pony that could pitch a cowboy into oblivion. As they raced to get alongside the herd, cowboys rode like lunatics through the dark, stormy night, intent on turning the herd. When it split apart into separate bunches in the dark, they couldn't see if they were chasing fifty cattle or several hundred. Every time the lightning flashed and lit up the darkness, they could see the steers crowded close together, whipping along like the devil was after them.

A stampede, like a prairie fire, was unwelcome, and riding pell-mell after a thundering herd was just asking for a short life. A cowboy had to think quickly and needed a good horse and plenty of good luck. If he was on a horse caught in the front or middle of a racing herd, the cattle might split and go around him. If he was on foot, he could be in trouble. One cowboy was so sleepy on night guard that he fell off his horse. He decided to take a short nap right there but awoke suddenly to the earth shaking beneath him and stampeding longhorns racing around him. His loyal horse was standing over him, protecting him on both sides from the trampling hoofs.

As they tried to stop a stampede, cowboys waved their hats and rain slickers, beat their ropes against their chaps, and fired their pistols into the ground to turn the animals. If they could turn the lead steers inward so they were running in a tight circle or "milling," it slowed the forward rush. As their circle tightened, the exhausted cattle would finally slow and stop.

James Cook, a Texas cowboy, had a hair-raising experience when he was racing with a herd across rough ground near a creek with high, steep banks. A flash of lightning lit up his surroundings, and Cook saw another cowboy and his horse leaping in midair, far out over the edge of the creek bank. Several cattle followed him, jumping to their certain death. Cook's horse didn't need a tug on the reins to stop his headlong rush forward. His mount braced his forefeet in the earth firmly enough to bring him to a sudden stop about five feet from the edge of the creek bank. The racing longhorns behind him suddenly turned so he wasn't pushed over the edge. The other cowboy who'd gone over the bluff was crushed beneath his horse and a dozen dead longhorns.

Two cowboys were chasing a stampeding herd when a bolt of lightning crashed so near that both were stunned. Another flash of lightning revealed one cowboy barely a foot from the edge of a steep chasm, while the other man's horse was sinking to his knees with his rider slumped in the saddle. They'd been struck by the bolt, and directly in front of the cowboy lay the herd's lead steer, which had been killed by that same bolt of lightning. Many stampeding cattle from the herd had raced blindly off the cliff, and most were dead in the gorge below. After a stampede, it didn't make any difference if the night was dark as coal with thunder and lightning popping all around—a cowboy's horse could get him back to camp.

A herd in flight could spread out over a vast area. If the cattle ran for twenty-five miles, the cowboys might have to ride two hundred miles rounding up the strays. Working alone, each man fanned out, flushed out runaways, and began pushing them toward the herd's new bedding ground. Sometimes small groups of cattle would be found and headed back toward the herd, but the most time was spent finding and driving single cows or steers back. If cattle from other trail herds were mixed into the stampede, it could take days to round them up and sort them out. Then the cattle might stampede again, and all that work would have to be done over.

Lightning took a toll, killing cowboys, their horses, and cattle on the plains, and there are many stories with tragic endings. In 1868, lightning struck a trail camp, killing one cowboy and severely burning two others. In 1870, a single bolt of lightning killed two cowboys who were taking shelter under a tree. The following year, lightning killed another cowboy near the Red River. When Ab Blocker was taking a herd of longhorns from Texas to Wyoming, a thunderstorm blew up about forty miles from Cheyenne. Lightning flashes lit up the sky as icy rain came down in buckets. The cook was handing out slickers to cowboys when a bolt of lightning struck nearby, knocking down five men and killing seven horses. Surprisingly, the cattle didn't stampede but rather moved about restlessly until the storm headed north, where it struck and killed one cowboy.

In recollections of his life as a cowpuncher in *We Pointed Them North*, Teddy Blue wrote about being struck by lightning twice. "The first time I heard thunder and then saw a fire ball coming toward me. I felt something strike me on the head. When I came to, I was lying under old Pete, and the rain was pouring down on my face. The second time, I was trying to get under a railroad bridge when it hit me, and I came to in the ditch. The cattle were always restless when there was a storm at night, even if it was a long way off, and that was when any little thing would start a run." Black cowboy Bob Leavitt was in a Colorado thunderstorm when a bolt of lightning struck the middle of the herd, killing six steers with one wallop and starting a stampede. There was always the danger of running off a cliff, or the next jump could land you in a shallow grave in a deep ravine.

On the day after a stampede, the exhausted cowboys, who'd been up all night, spent the day rounding up cattle, driving them back to the herd, and tallying up their numbers. That night, the cattle were quiet and the cowboys were asleep in their blanket rolls until around 4:00 a.m., when the cook lit the fire to get coffee going and the herd took off again. The cook, Jeff, jumped up on the chuck wagon tongue, waving a blanket and yelling, "Boys! Boys! Stampede!" The cowboys jumped out of their blankets and ran to their horses. One man had just gotten his foot in the stirrup when the cattle knocked him to the ground and roared past. Hours later, the stampede was stopped, and several steers were dead, their necks broken when the others ran right over them. The boys returned to camp and found the unfortunate cowboy groaning on the ground. The cattle hadn't hurt him, but he'd landed in a big patch of prickly pear cactus. After the others finally got him extracted from the thorns, the cook spent hours probing his painful wounds with pinchers by lantern light.

Sometimes a single troublemaking steer could cause repeated stampedes. If he was identified, the trail boss would trade him off, or he'd end up in the stew pot. In 1871, John Chisum was driving six thousand longhorns from his Texas ranch to his new headquarters at Roswell. Following directly behind him on the Goodnight-Loving Trail was another herd of three thousand steers that had been stampeding every night. They'd smashed the chuck wagon, dumped all the supplies, and were skin and bones from running, yet they still stampeded. The cowboys were worn out and puzzled about the cause of the nightly panic. John Chisum offered to help their trail boss by sending his right-hand man, Black cowboy Frank Chisum, to see if he could pinpoint the cause. As the steers were bedding down that evening, Frank rode slowly through the herd, looking at each animal carefully. Then he called out to the trail boss, "There's the cause of your stampedes." He pointed out a spotted, lanky steer that was "narrow between the eyes with corkscrew horns and one-eyed." Frank said, "He can't see, and he doesn't have any sense besides." The steer was disposed of, and the stampedes stopped. The trail boss and his cowboys praised Frank as a "real cowman" who'd spotted the troublemaker that had been causing their three thousand steers to stampede nightly.

Black cowboy Addison Jones was with a crew driving a large herd up the Goodnight-Loving Trail through Colorado. The longhorns were stampeding every night, and everyone was worn out. One bitter cold night, when he was on night guard, Old Ad was walking around the herd and leading his horse to keep from freezing. He spotted a big white steer standing up while the other cattle were quietly lying down. Suddenly, the steer leaped into the air and came down with a heavy thud, hitting the ground with his nose and giving a loud grunt. Immediately, the entire herd was on its feet and running, heading straight for Jones. His frightened horse jerked loose and ran away, and he had just enough time to scramble up a tree as the cattle raced by, striking the tree with their horns. The crazed cattle ran all night before the cowboys got them turned back, and it took the next day to round them up. When the white steer was pointed out, the trail boss traded the troublemaker to an Indian, and there were no more stampedes.

Black cowboy John Sneed, who'd ridden the Goodnight-Loving and Chisolm Trails many times with Ab Blocker, and Jed Brackenridge, pioneer Texas cattleman, told a WPA worker for the *Slave Narratives* about a memorable stampede. "I rode 24 hours straight and after we rounded up the cattle, I goes to sleep under a tree." Sneed was wearing a heavy buckskin coat and was suddenly awakened. "I feel somethin' grab dat coat and bite my side. I rouses up and see a big panther draggin' me off to de thicket." He had a six-gun, but he couldn't reach it. He said, "Every once in a while dat' panther lay me down and sniff at my nose. I jes hold de breath 'cause if dat panther cotch me breathin', dat be de end of me." Sneed said the panther dragged him to the bushes, went off a little bit, and gave a loud scream. He said, "Dat yell turned me cold 'cause it sound jes' like a man screamin'. Den dat cat dug a shallow hole. I eases out my old gun, takes careful aim, and den says, 'Thank you, old man,' and he turns to look at me, and I shoots him right between de eyes." Then Sneed said he killed the lion's mate and cubs when they came to dine on his carcass.

The cattle drive ended successfully at the railhead after the steers were in the stock pens waiting shipment or were loaded into the railroad cars. One night in Kansas, clouds were gathering, but the wind was light and the cowhands watching the longhorns in the stock pens weren't worried about a storm. Then there was a sudden clap of thunder announcing that a storm had suddenly blown up. Down went the stockyard fences and out streamed the cattle. A cowboy named Jim told the WPA worker for the *Slave Narratives*, "I got the general direction they were heading and tried to get in front of them. Rode about two miles and heard them coming 7–8 abreast down a draw in front of me. They would have to cross the creek that would slow 'em up. I hurried ahead to where they'd cross and cut off the ones that had already crossed, and it was some time before the tail of the herd caught up. I held them all on a flat until morning, and when the boys came, we counted and were about two hundred short. We found them about four miles further where they'd gone into another herd headed for New Mexico. We didn't lose any cows—just energy cutting them out and taking them back to the corrals."

Stampedes could kill or injure cowboys. Cattle could be crushed, run over by others, dash off a cliff, or drown in a river. When cattle stampeded, their nervousness spread, and they ran senselessly night after night until they were exhausted and lost weight. On a hot night, a steer that ran ten miles could lose up to forty pounds. Fat steers that stampeded often became ghosts of their former selves.

COOKIE RULES

For years, every cowboy on a cattle drive carried a tin can or coffee pot, a small pan, roasted coffee, jerky, salt pork, and cold biscuits in a flour sack behind his saddle. At the end of a long day in the saddle, often too tired to fix a simple meal, he'd grab a biscuit and jerky, brew strong coffee, and fall into his bedroll for a few hours of sleep before it was time to ride night herd. On drives to supply beef to the Confederacy, some cattlemen took a slave to cook and carried supplies on a mule for his "greasy sack outfit." A clumsy, slow, ox-drawn cart was used on longer drives and usually reached the evening bedding ground long after the trail crew, delaying the evening meal.

Charles Goodnight designed the first chuck wagon as a good way to feed the cowboys driving his cattle to New Mexico. He rebuilt a durable, army surplus Studebaker wagon and replaced its wooden axles with iron ones that would hold up on rugged terrain. He built a large chuck box on the back of the wagon with shelves and deep drawers for tin plates, cups, cutlery or "eatin irons," salt, and pepper. Its hinged lid made a good work area for the cook and served as a kitchen table. Larger compartments held bags of flour, coffee, sugar, beans, and dried fruit, while the Dutch oven, larger pots, and skillets were stored in the boot beneath. Other deep drawers held a five-gallon keg of sourdough starter, a slab of salt pork, onions, potatoes, cans of tomatoes, and jugs of molasses, called "lick," that were packed well and tied down. There was a drawer for bandages and medicinal remedies: quinine, calomel (a laxative), black draught, sewing supplies, and liniment for use on man and beast.

The chuck wagon on a Texas roundup, circa 1900. *William Henry Jackson, Library of Congress.*

A water barrel with a spigot and the coffee mill were attached to the outside of the wagon with cowhide. On the opposite side of the wagon was a box with an axe, branding irons, a shovel, and grain for the mules. Some wagons had a jockey box in front to store hobbles, heavier tools, and a barrel of whiskey for snakebites. Underneath the wagon was a hammock, called the "cooney" from Spanish *cuna* meaning cradle. It was also known as the "possum belly" and held wood and buffalo or cow chips. Waterproof sheets of canvas were stretched over the wagon bows to keep everything dry. A "fly" or canvas awning was attached to the top of the chuck box and rolled out to shelter the cook when it rained. The wagon had wide tires for better traction, and the wagon bed had extra sideboards to hold the cowboys' bedrolls and possessions. The wagon was drawn by a yoke of six sturdy oxen or mules. Many cattlemen quickly adopted the chuck wagon, and some even included a second wagon to store cowboys' bedrolls and possessions, spare saddles, hammer, axe, shovel, feed for horses, bulk food supplies, additional water, and medical supplies. Called the hooligan wagon, this was usually driven by the night hawk, or an extra night wrangler. The chuck wagon greatly improved the life of cowboys on the trail and at roundups.

Once a cattleman had a chuck wagon, he needed a cook, who was usually hired by the trail boss. Often a veteran cowhand got the job. Very few cooks were young, and sometimes they were "stove up" old cowboys, limping about with reminders of unfortunate encounters with broncs or steers. Although their bodies rebelled at sixteen-hour days in the saddle, they didn't want to leave the trail, and the chuck wagon offered an alternative. There was never a surplus supply of cooks, and experienced ones were in great demand. If a cook came along, it was common to hire him a few months ahead of a trail drive and pay him wages. Some cooks were added to the payroll out of desperation because there were no other candidates for the job. They knew little about cooking—as the crew unhappily learned. Others weren't on good terms with the law and spent a lot of time looking over their shoulders. The cook was second in authority to the trail boss and earned about sixty to seventy-five dollars per month.

The cook was important on a cattle drive and at the ranch. Cowboys might like everything about an outfit—their wages, their boss, the working conditions—but if the cook turned out poor meals, they grew discontented and irritable. A cook who consistently produced good food was appreciated by a contented, hardworking crew and the boss.

On a cattle drive, the cook was responsible for preparing the meals, safeguarding the food supplies, and taking care of the cowboys' bedrolls and possessions stored in the chuck wagon. The cook had to be able to turn out a meal in a dust storm, a blizzard, a cloud burst, or a high wind. The cook was the crew's doctor dispensing home remedies, the dentist who'd pull a tooth with pliers, the banker who held the winnings from card games and bets, and a confessor listening to a cowhand's complaints and laments.

Cowboys were slow to criticize cooks who lacked culinary talent but kept their pots and pans clean, scoured them with sand and wood ashes, always wore a clean apron, and didn't have dirty fingernails. They were inclined to forgive a cook who was as fussy as an old maid about serving up clean food, and they approved of one who guarded his cooking pots and forbade any cowboy from dipping his personal spoon in for "just a taste."

When preparing for the trail drive, the chuck wagon, pots and pans, the Dutch oven, utensils, and water barrel were given a thorough scrubbing. The sourdough keg was vigorously cleaned and aired in the sun. The harnesses were checked so they were in good condition, the wagon axles were greased, and all repairs were made before the cooking utensils and food supplies were carefully packed. There was a place for everything, and perishables like salt pork were loaded just before leaving. Empty flour sacks were taken apart and used as aprons and dish towels and stowed in the wagon along with plenty of soap and one or two huge wreck pans (dish pans). The cowboys eyed the spotless chuck wagon and cooking gear with satisfaction because they could see that Old Cookie lived up to his reputation for cleanliness. There was always hope that he could cook beans and steaks and turn out light, fluffy sourdough biscuits.

The cook ruled the chuck wagon and about sixty square feet surrounding it. The trail boss was careful about giving orders around the chuck wagon, as this was the cook's domain—even the cattle owner walked softly here. Many cowpunchers viewed the cook as cranky and crusty, warning, "Crossin' a cook is as risky as brandin' a mule's tail." Many chuck wagon cooks had bad tempers and relished their nasty reputations as tyrants around camp. Cowboys didn't complain because they didn't want the cook to take revenge on them or quit in a fit of temper. Revenge on the crew might take the form of weak coffee, gravel in the beans, or biscuits burned or hard as rocks and served with tough, gristly steaks. An unfortunate cowboy who drew the cook's ire might find his bedroll missing or soaking wet, his spare clothes and few possessions misplaced as he endured a series of mishaps. While some cooks were bad-tempered despots described by one cowboy as "hard featured and unlovely," most Black cooks were easier to get along with than their white counterparts. Many had grown up around plantation or ranch kitchens and could cook well.

Just as there were nasty cooks, there were many more who helped make a happy camp and even joined the cowboys' boisterous fun. Most Black workers had been slaves or the children of slaves and knew their way around the barn and stables and cared for livestock as youngsters. Many apprenticed as wranglers, became cowboys in their teens, and had plenty of experience on the ranch and cattle drives. Presiding over the ranch kitchen or chuck wagon gave the Black cook prestige and a higher wage, but he was at the top of his promotion ladder. An ambitious white cook had a chance to become ranch foreman or trail boss, but the Black cook did not.

The chuck wagon was the center of the cattle drive, and it represented home. While feeding the cowboys was his primary responsibility, the cook could do a lot toward making life more pleasant for everyone around him. A cowboy's decision to sign on with a cattle drive was often based on who was presiding over the chuck wagon. A good-natured, bustling cook meant a lot to the trail boss and the cowboys. The cook's cheerful voice calling out at daybreak, "Roll out there, fellers and hear the little birdies sing their praises

George Jackson, cowboy cook on right, with D.J. O'Malley standing at cook tent in Montana cow camp. *Montana Historical Society.*

to God!" or "Arise and shine and give glory to the Lord!" would make the most crusty cowboy smile as he crawled out of his blankets for breakfast.

Cowboys had nicknames for their cooks like "Cookie" or "Coosie," from the Spanish *cocinero* for cook. The cook was also referred to as the biscuit roller, bean master, belly cheater, dough wrangler, greasy belly, pot rustler, sourdough, and even as the old lady. No one ever used an uncomplimentary name to his face.

Cooking over a campfire was not easy under the best conditions, but the cook knew that cowboys needed hot food during cold, wet weather. Keeping the fire going and hot enough to cook was often quite challenging. A soaking rainstorm could quickly douse the fire, or cold winds would blow the flames everywhere but at the Dutch oven or coffee pot. A sudden breeze might toss sand into the simmering contents when a pot lid was lifted. Despite the numerous aggravations presented by the weather, there was always the possibility of the chuck wagon breaking an axle or getting mired in a bottomless mud hole.

The cook was up before dawn every morning to get the fire started, coffee made, and breakfast ready before the wrangler brought in the remuda. Many cooks didn't carry timepieces of any sort and judged the time of day by the sun. They were fairly accurate, even on cloudy days, and usually had meals on time. Some cooks carried an alarm clock, which they set to go off before dawn. Each evening, the cook wound the alarm and put the clock on a tin plate or an overturned bucket so when the alarm went off, the irritating clatter woke the men. Other cooks simply roused the sleeping cowboys by yelling loudly, "Rise 'n shine, boys! Come 'n git it!" or "Roll out! Roll out! While she's hot!"

Morning, noon, and night, there was always plenty of strong black coffee and sourdough biscuits. A large coffee pot, usually three to five gallons for twelve to fifteen men, boiled away on the campfire coals. Coffee was essential to the cowboy. He wanted coffee at every meal and readily available between meals when he was in camp. He needed a cup of hot coffee when he was going out to ride night herd and a cup when he returned to camp before crawling into his blankets for a few hours of sleep. If the coffee wasn't strong enough, there was plenty of grumbling. Cowboys didn't use any milk, cream, or sweetener in their coffee. One cowboy summed it up: "This is the way I like it—plumb barefoot. None of that dehorned stuff you git in town!" They always complained that restaurant coffee was too weak, calling it "belly wash" or "brown gargle."

Arbuckles Coffee was the preferred brand, and every ranch kept several cases on hand. After the Civil War, the Arbuckle brothers developed a process for roasting coffee beans and glazing them to seal in their flavor and aroma. Demand for this coffee became overwhelming, and cases were shipped all over the country. The cook always loaded plenty of Arbuckles into the chuck wagon, and when he had a chance, the wrangler ground twenty to thirty bags of beans so plenty of coffee was ready.

Sourdough biscuits were standard fare at most meals, and cowboys were critical connoisseurs. They preferred sourdough biscuits over those made with baking powder. Every cook wanted to be known for his light, fluffy biscuits and protected his methods jealously. Cowboys grumbled about the bread they were served in town restaurants, calling it "wasp nest bread" or "gun wadding bread."

The cast-iron Dutch oven, used for generations, was indispensable as the cook turned out sourdough biscuits, cobblers, and stews. This large, deep pot with three short legs was designed for cooking on an open hearth or over a campfire. It sat in the coals, with more coals piled around its sides and on top of its flat, tightly fitting lid.

Cowhands didn't have to be called twice for meals, and many claimed to be "hungry enough to eat their blankets." They hurriedly grabbed their plates, cups, and eatin' irons and lined up to serve themselves. Breakfast usually included sourdough biscuits, slab pork or bacon, and stewed apples, raisins, or prunes. They ate hunkered down or sitting on the ground with their plates on their laps or bedrolls. When they finished, the dirty dishes and utensils were piled into the wreck pan for washing. While the cowboys ate, the cook and the wrangler washed the dishes, packed the chuck wagon, hitched up the team, and were ready to pull out ahead of the herd.

Dinner was the popular name for the midday meal, which usually included sourdough biscuits and beef in some form. Vegetables were canned, with corn and thirst-quenching tomatoes the favorites. While the men ate, the cattle grazed, and when the cows began to lie down, the trail boss got the herd on its feet and moving.

In the late afternoon, when the cook reached the camping spot for the night, he pulled the chuck wagon off the trail and began preparations for supper. The wrangler unhitched and watered the team and gathered firewood. Supper was the highlight of the cowboys' day. There was always beef served in different ways: beef roasts, ribs, or steaks rolled in flour and fried in bacon fat in the Dutch oven. There might be a beef stew with plenty of potatoes and onions in a rich gravy that the cowboys mopped up with sourdough biscuits. Sometimes a yearling steer was traded to a local farmer for fresh corn, beans, or peas from his garden. If there was time, the cook might make a dessert for the boys, usually a fruit pie or cobbler. Bread pudding loaded with raisins or sweetened, stewed tomatoes baked with biscuit dough were favorites. When cooks began including rice in their menus, they put together a quick dessert called "John Chinaman" or "Spotted Pup" by adding raisins and cinnamon to cooked rice. Occasionally, a cowboy might find bird or duck eggs and take them to the cook to be whipped into a delicious dessert.

When the trail boss decided that the cattle needed a day or two to rest, cowboys would go hunting for dinner for a change from their usual diet of beef. Sometimes a valley near a river would be covered with wild turkeys roosting in cottonwood trees. Huge flocks of ducks and geese darkened the sky overhead, herds of elusive antelope raced across the grasslands, and there was an occasional buffalo. If the cowboys had a successful hunt, supper plates would be piled high with delicious venison, roast turkey, duck, antelope steaks, or even a buffalo hump roast. Cowboys liked young turkeys fried like chicken and often went out hunting turkey nests, returning with turkey eggs. The damp bottomlands were overgrown with wild berries, crab apples, chokecherries, and wild plums, which made flavorful pies and cobblers. The cowboy who picked the fruit was sure to be rewarded with an extra serving.

Pecan trees grew wild in Texas, and the giant trees were loaded with nuts in the fall. The cowboy who took off his shirt and filled it with pecans saw everyone rewarded with molasses-pecan pies spiced with bourbon.

Most of the rivers and lakes were full of fish, and the anglers in the crew provided plenty for big fish fries. Old Jeff was often the cook on Tobe Odem's cattle drives up the Chisholm Trail to Dodge City. Along the way, there was plenty of game, and the streams were so full of fish that a man could just reach in and grab one. It didn't take long to "catch" enough for a big fish fry. All the cowboys pitched in to clean the catch, which Old Jeff rolled in cornmeal and fried in bacon fat for "plenty of fine eatin'." Everyone liked Jeff, whose only complaint was about the chuck wagon. Rubbing his backside, he'd say, "This old wagon sho' bumps powerful bad, and Jeff's bones kinda rusty now." He'd say, "If you boys ever come on a buffalo, please git me some of that hair to sit on."

One morning, before they got on the trail, the camp was startled by a barrage of gunshots, and everyone was sure that a gun battle with the

The chuck wagon, "Sour Dough for Dinner," circa 1908. *Erwin E. Smith, National Cowboy & Western Heritage Museum.*

roaming Comanches was underway. The cowboys quickly saddled their fastest horses, grabbed extra ammunition, and galloped off to find the fight. A few miles west of the herd, they crested a hill to see that it wasn't Indians shooting—it was buffalo hunters slaughtering the animals for their hides. In those days, a buffalo hide brought four dollars apiece, and after skinning, the carcasses were left to rot on the prairie.

The disgusted crew didn't join in the killing, saying, "It's a shame to kill them critters for hides that sell for so little!" They harvested several buffalo humps to take to Old Jeff, and remembering the cook's request, they cut a lot of the long, curly hair off the buffalo heads and filled gunnysacks with it. This hair was selling for one dollar per sack, and it could be twisted into strings and made into saddle cinches and bridle reins. Old Jeff was really pleased with the hair and made a fine, fat pillow to cushion his old bones. As thanks to the boys, he roasted a buffalo hump and made "a passel" of wild plum pies for their dessert.

Many cowboys who worked in the brush country of southern Texas had fond memories of a gentle, good-natured cook known as Sam. Writer J. Frank Dobie in his book *Vaquero of the Brush Country* recorded cowboy John Young's memories of Sam: "The one man in our outfit that I recall most often and most vividly was Sam, the Negro cook. He always had a cheerful word or a happy song, and he seemed to have an affection for every one of us. When we camped in the vicinity of the brush, every cowboy coming in from the trail would rope a chunk of wood and snake it up to the chuck wagon. The wood always made Sam grinning happy, whether he needed it or not." Sam was a good all-around cowboy too, but when he was thirty-five years old and weighed 225 pounds, he decided that he was a little too heavy and a little too old to continue that life. He had a knack for cooking, and that was the crew's good fortune. Occasionally, a cowboy asked him to put aside his pots and pans and "top off" an unruly wild horse because he was such a skilled rider. Sam was always agreeable, and after the horse had bucked around under Sam's bulk a while, the bronc called it a day and settled down.

Sam enjoyed cooking, and whether he was on the trail or at the ranch, he turned out luscious meals the likes of which no one had seen before. When a camp was established long enough for the cowboys to hunt, Sam would create his famous "wedding feast," a combined dinner and supper of barbecued antelope ribs, buffalo steaks, or roast wild turkey. On those special occasions, the crew washed their faces, combed their hair, and waited eagerly for Sam to call out, "Come and get it while she's hot and juicy!"

After the dishes were washed, it didn't take much to coax Sam into picking some favorites on his banjo as the crew relaxed around the campfire. When one of the cowboys accidentally stepped on his banjo and broke it, everyone chipped in and bought him a violin. Sam quickly learned to play this new instrument, and at night he sawed away or picked out popular tunes for his enthusiastic audience.

The herd provided beef, which was wrapped in cloth and covered with blankets to keep it cool. A side of beef didn't last long around the trail crew, who were always ready to eat. Just as sourdough biscuits were a test of the cook's ability, son of a gun stew was another. The less refined name for this very old stew from the cattle country was S.O.B. stew, made after an animal was slaughtered. This cowboy favorite was made with cubed pieces of tongue, heart, tenderloin, sweetbreads, brains, and offal, parts of organs and viscera trimmings. Chopped onion, salt, and chili powder were added, and the mixture was cooked for several hours. Old-timers swore that a good amount of chopped marrow gut, the milk-secreting tract found in calves, was essential, and brains were cooked separately and added before the stew was served.

After the dishes were done, the wrangler filled the water barrel and stacked wood by the campfire for the morning. Before the cook wearily rolled up in his blankets, he pointed the chuck wagon's tongue toward the North Star as a compass for the trail boss the following morning.

The cook always worried about having enough fuel on hand to cook meals. Hardwood was ideal because it burned longer, gave off more heat, and made hotter coals. However, hardwood wasn't always available, and the cook might have to settle for pine or buffalo or cow chips. These dried manure piles made a hot fire but burned up quickly, and a lot were needed. Cow chips had an unpleasant odor when they burned, and if they were damp, they'd hardly burn at all. When a fire was slow to start, the cook would fan the flames with his hat, but by the end of the season, he'd need new head gear. One cook commented wryly, "I wore out three good hats tryin' to get the danged cow chips to burn!" Maintaining the wood or cow chip supply fell to the wrangler, and everyone knew that their meals depended on adequate fuel. When a cowboy saw a log or piece of good wood, he'd rope it and "snake it" back to camp.

Even though they lived and worked on the range far from the city, cowboys wanted some order and courtesy in their world. They had a code and followed certain rules in the way they conducted themselves and treated others. There was no better place to see this than during a meal around the campfire. Consideration of others was obvious in everyone's actions, and this maintained a peaceful camp.

COOK'S RULES
1. Never tie your horse to the chuck wagon.
2. No one eats until cookie calls.
3. There's no pushing or rushing.
4. Avoid getting dirt or sand into the food in the Dutch oven.
5. Refill others' coffee cups when you refill yours.
6. Don't take the last piece unless you're sure everyone else has enough.
7. It's OK to eat with your fingers.
8. Scrape your dishes and stack them in the wreck pan.
9. Help replenish the wood supply.
10. Strangers are always welcome.

The cowboys were lucky if their cook had a friendly disposition like Sam or Jim Perry, who made life on the trail more pleasant. Evenings around the campfire with these cooks were often filled with tall tales and jokes, bawdy ballads, or melodies played on the fiddle. A cook who occasionally hummed a tune over his pots might be coaxed into singing a dirty ditty or a mournful melody, while Big Jim Simpson or Sam would play a lonely lament on a musical instrument. Wash Adams, a cook for the XIT Ranch, often sang old plantation songs like "Oh, Mary, My Mary" in a rich baritone as he stirred his pots. These cooks usually provided the music for special celebrations and Saturday night dances during the winter when cowboys were at the ranches.

There's not much information about Big Jim Simpson, a Black cowboy who came to Wyoming from Texas with Joe Proctor on a cattle drive. He was a talented roper, and in the 1880s, he had a reputation as one of the best in Wyoming. Jim was always welcome when he hired on to a trail crew, first as a cowboy and later as a cook. He was a wise friend and advisor to young cowboys and even listened to their romance problems. His experiences on the hazards encountered on the trail made him an expert teacher for young greenhorns on their first cattle drive.

When one of the crew became sick from drinking alkali water, Jim took care of him, putting him on a strict diet of tomato juice until his symptoms subsided. Jim Simpson and Joe Proctor, who was also Black, worked at the Flying E Ranch near Greybull, Wyoming. Jim was a good cook and sometimes took over the chuck wagon on cattle drives. He often played for "kitchen dances," which were held in the only space available, a ranch or farm kitchen. An accomplished fiddle player, his renditions of popular songs, lively jigs, polkas, and romantic waltzes had everyone on the dance floor on Saturday nights. The space was usually so cramped that only four couples could dance at the same time, but everyone had a rousing good time. Jim played until dawn, when everyone sat down together and shared a big breakfast and then headed home.

During the winter, Jim was always welcome in the homes of his numerous Black and white friends. He spent at least two winters at the George Harper ranch helping Mrs. Harper, a young mother who had cut her hand badly. The wound became infected, and she developed blood poisoning and became critically ill; she had her hand amputated to save her life. Jim stepped in while she was recuperating from surgery and took care of her four young children. He managed the household, cooking, cleaning, washing, and even mending the children's clothing. Jim's help was invaluable to the Harper family, and his kindness brought him even more friends.

Floyd Bard, whose family had a small ranch near Greybull, ran away to be a cowboy when he was thirteen. He was hired to wrangle horses at the RL Ranch and remembered George, the Black cowboy, who cooked there. He was known for his friendly ways and kindness to drifters, who appreciated a hot supper and maybe a warm bed in the bunkhouse. George was famous for baking cakes that were feather light and juicy fruit pies with flaky crusts.

In 1897, young Floyd Bard got a job as George's helper at a large spring roundup. Bard described this four-day event in his book, *Horse Wrangler: Sixty Years in the Saddle*. George set up three tables to serve meals to more than forty cowboys. He had a large cooking fire with plenty of Dutch ovens, several coffee pots and cast-iron skillets where he cooked three meals a day for the hungry men. Floyd kept the fire going and washed mountains of dishes for George, whose good disposition kept everyone laughing and joking despite the hard work.

When he was cooking in the ranch house, George always wore a clean apron and kept an immaculate kitchen. Floyd was his favorite helper, and he often saved special treats for the boy and let him have extra helpings of dessert. When Floyd was wrangling horses for a roundup at another ranch and George was hired as cook, he always set aside special goodies for the youth, grinning as he said, "Boss, how about this nice piece of pie or cake? Saved it just for you."

Some chuck wagon cooks turned out meals that were remembered for decades: sourdough biscuits that floated in beef gravy, tasty son of a gun stew, and bread pudding full of raisins and sweetened with molasses. Other

Group of Black cowboys on horses, stock hands of Thomas W. Jones, 1880s. Jones is standing in the foreground. The third cowboy from left is holding the TJ brand of Thomas Jones (1840–1895), son of George Ranch founder Henry Jones. *George Ranch Historical Park.*

cooks were known for their tough steaks, weak coffee, and rocks they called biscuits. One French Black cook named Zeno achieved fame of a sort in 1872 because of an accident. He kept baking soda in a wide-mouthed pickle jar and calomel, "the universal laxative," in another jar just like it. When he was making bread, Zeno accidentally grabbed the calomel jar, and it went into the bread. A cowboy later wrote, "All the cowboys ate the bread despite 'its peculiar taste'" and recalled, "We were sure a sick lot!"

Chuck wagon cooks can't be given too much praise. Years ago, an anonymous cattleman wrote in the *Prescott Courier*, "A roundup cook is a sort of human that was kicked in the head by a brindle cow or a cross-grained mule when very young. This leaves him clear and accounts for the line of work he does. Nobody with good sense could be a good roundup cook and nobody unless they're queer kin do it. Takes a special talent to wrangle a Dutch oven and feed 15 or 20 men that eat like walruses all hours of the day or night, ride through wind and dirt, snow and cold rain and mud an git the job done. They're temperamental as wimmin, too; an' like the bosses don't need no sleep neither. Also, they is very cranky. The breed is fast dyin' out; they can't stand domesticatin'.'"

THE TRAIL DRIVE ENDS IN TOWN

It was the end of the trail! The buildings of Abilene could be seen in the distance, with the stockyards and railroad depot, and the tired cowboys, cheered by the sight, broke into yells and whoops. Finally, after months of irritable steers, stampedes, dust, mud, storms, rain and wind, dangerous river crossings, Indians, rustlers, and long days and nights in the saddle, they'd reached their destination. They were ready to celebrate—to make up for all those hard days and sleepless nights on the trail. They wanted some fun!

Straight ahead there were saloons where liquor flowed freely and gambling tables where they could risk their earnings at monte, faro, or poker. There were dance halls with the prettiest women to dance with and bawdy houses with their flocks of soiled doves. There were hotels with beds and clean sheets and restaurants where they'd sit in chairs and eat at a table, where steaks would be served on china without grit and sand, and they'd be eaten with silver knives and forks. There were baths where they could wash away months of grime from the trail and get a shave and a much-needed haircut. Stores lined the streets where they could buy new clothes and boots to replace shirts and pants worn thin. The cowboys could hardly wait. But first the cattle had to be counted and sold while the sights of Abilene and a good time waited.

The townspeople welcomed the young cowboys with their wallets full of money earned by hard months on the trail. True, they didn't like the

Dodge City, Kansas, circa 1878. A boomtown destination of cattle drives on Chisholm Trail. The peak years were 1883–84 in this "Queen of the Cow Towns" as thousands of longhorns passed through its stockyards annually. *Robert Marr Wright (1840–1915), Collections of the University of California Libraries.*

carousing and loud nights when the cowboys were drunk and determined to shoot up the town. But they realized that these young men had followed the herds for a thousand miles or more, had rarely seen a house, a garden, women, or children for many tedious months. Now they needed some entertainment, and for want of anything better, they'd find it in the saloons and gambling halls.

These cowboys had encountered all kinds of danger and trouble on the trail, and many would learn that trouble lurked in town too. There were crooked gamblers, cheating shop keepers, shifty saloon bartenders, and sneaky soiled doves, all intent on emptying their wallets of their hard-earned cash. There was something else cowboys coming to town for the first time hadn't expected: the discrimination their Black companions would face. In the 1870s and 1880s, Black cowboys were common on the trail, and there was an equality among members of trail drive crews. Every man was judged on his character and the work he could do, but when they all rode into town, things changed. While citizens welcomed the white cowboys, many ignored the Black men, letting them know that they weren't welcome and would not get equal treatment.

This prejudice was quickly noticed by most cowboys. Usually, cowboys got along well on cattle drives, worked together, appreciated their differences, and respected their good qualities. There were seldom visitors on the trail, and cowboys entertained one another with jokes and funny stories, card games, and bets. If there was a practical joker in the crew, anybody could become a victim of his tricks.

In town, restaurants and hotel dining rooms often refused to seat or serve the Black cowboys, but some would allow them to eat in the kitchen. After sharing meals around the campfire for months, this open discrimination did not sit well with many white cowboys. When one man questioned a manager about his refusal to serve his Black companion, he was informed, "It was the rules." The white cowboy snapped, "Well, your rules have changed!" and pulled his six-shooter. The group of cowboys, including the Black man, were quickly served.

Some hotels would not rent rooms to Black cowboys, and they often received a cool reception in saloons, where they could not buy a drink. If the establishment agreed to sell a Black cowboy a shot of whiskey, he'd usually have to drink it standing at the far end of the bar. He could expect to be questioned aggressively about his presence, and he might be taunted or insulted. There was a threat of potential violence in every encounter a Black cowboy had with white citizens. White men always entertained the age-old fear that Black cowboys would try to patronize the town's white prostitutes. This didn't happen because Black men knew that it would cause trouble. Some towns had brothels with one or more Black ladies of the evening, and a few towns had an establishment with Black women that catered only to Black men.

Seeing the unfair way their friends were treated, some white cowboys stood with their Black companions, refusing to drink in segregated saloons or walking out together when a restaurant refused to serve the Black members of their group. Some Black cowboys even chose to forego the big celebration in town at the end of the trail and remained in camp. They did not want the trouble that discrimination could bring or cast a pall on their celebration.

Jeff was the Black cook for a cattle drive run by Tobe Odem from Texas to Dodge City in 1877. At the end of the drive, Jeff rode into town with the others, but after getting two or three drinks with his friends and seeing no other Black people, Jeff decided to go back to camp. He bought a quart of whiskey, loaded supplies for the camp, saddled his horse, and left. The following morning, when the other cowboys came straggling into camp much the worse for wear, Jeff had the coffee pot on the fire and sourdough biscuits in the Dutch oven.

Gordon Davis, a Black cowboy, occasionally cooked on Ab Blocker's cattle drives to Montana and often livened up the evenings playing the boys' favorite tunes on his fiddle. When an especially long, difficult drive finally reached Dodge City, the cowboys were elated and headed for town to celebrate. Gordon joined them and made a spectacular entrance by riding down Main Street on one of the oxen that usually pulled his chuck wagon. As a crowd clapped and cheered, he even provided his own musical fanfare as he tucked his violin under his chin and played "Buffalo Gal Won't You Come Out Tonight?"

Abilene had become a wild, rowdy town full of rambunctious cowboys and pens of bawling cattle by 1870. The town's first jail was being completed under a heavy guard after some Texas cowboys had pulled down its walls weeks earlier. The Black cook of a Texas crew that was camped outside Abilene rode into town to drown his thirst with the boys. Unfortunately, he drank too much and began shooting up the place. Bullets were flying, but luckily, no one was hurt; however, the marshal was upset. He arrested the cook and threw him in jail, where he spent the night contemplating the error of his ways.

The next morning, when the cowboys rolled out of their blankets, there was no coffee pot boiling away on the fire and breakfast wasn't ready. To make matters worse, their cook was missing. The hungry, disgruntled crew rode into town to find him languishing in jail. They chased the marshal away, shot the new lock off the jailhouse door, and rescued the cook. Then they galloped past the town hall and shot it full of holes to show their contempt for local government. Their Black cook had set a record: he was the first to be thrown into the new jail, and he was the first man to break out.

In the 1870s and 1880s, the range cattle business was booming, and Cheyenne became the financial and social center. Cattleman Bill Walker brought a large herd of cattle to sell at the railhead and paid his cowboys in advance. The crew, with money in their pockets, headed into Cheyenne for some fun in the saloons, poker joints, and dance halls. The town had only one real street, but it boasted a clothing store with a large plate glass window, which the cowboys used as a mirror, admiring themselves in their new duds.

The Black cook, Bronco Sam, who was known as a "genuine Black buckaroo" and wasn't afraid of anything, had joined the celebration. After three wild days in town, the crew straggled back to camp. Few were sober and their pockets were empty, but they wanted one more last fling in town that would give Cheyenne something to remember. The crew

Black cowboys posing for photograph in wooly chaps, circa 1913. *Grant-Kohrs Ranch National Historic Site.*

Kansas-Pacific Railroad locomotive. Cattle were driven to shipping points in Kansas once railroad lines were completed. *DeGolyer Library, Southern Methodist University.*

cleaned up, roped the biggest steer in the herd, and managed to get a saddle on him. Sam, who wasn't any more sober than the rest, climbed aboard. They headed back to town, whooping and hollering, intending to have their Black bronc buster ride the steer down Cheyenne's Main Street. By the time they got to town, the frantic steer was furious, and then he saw his reflection in the store's plate glass window. With a mighty bellow, the steer charged right through the window, loped down the aisles, jumped over the counters, and dashed around the shelves. Sales clerks dived into corners while the steer plunged through the clothing racks, and then it charged back outside through the empty window frame.

Sam was still in the saddle, and the steer's horns were decorated with underwear, pants, coats, hats, and other odds and ends. The steer jumped and bucked about as Sam shouted loudly, "I brought out a new suit of clothes for everybody!" The cowboys headed the bucking steer back to the herd and helped the buckaroo dismount. Later, when they'd all sobered up, Sam and his friends rode back to town, where they got an unfriendly reception from the store manager. Sam was all smiles and politely announced that he'd pay for the damages. Now that was different, so the manager quickly made a long list. When he told Sam that the total damages were $350, the cowboy never batted an eye; he peeled off the greenbacks and handed them over. Then Sam and the crew waved goodbye and rode proudly out of Cheyenne.

Cowboys worked together, surviving challenges and difficult situations, and they were fiercely loyal to their outfits. In his autobiography, cowboy Nat Love recalled the camaraderie of cowboys with admiration. "A braver, truer set of men never lived than these wild sons of the plains whose home was in the saddle and their couch, Mother Earth, with the sky for a covering," he wrote. "They were always ready to share their blanket and their last ration with a less fortunate fellow companion and always assisted each other in the many trying situations that were continually coming up in a cowboy's life."

LIFE ON THE RANCH

Most Black cowboys had been taking care of horses and cattle since they were children and knew how to ride and work on a ranch. While some cowboys were driving cattle to the railroads for shipment to eastern markets, others stayed at the ranch, caring for the herds and maintaining operations. Tom Mills, born enslaved in Alabama, told the WPA interviewer for the *Slave Narratives* that he'd been working with cattle for fifty years. "Many a year passed that I never missed a day in the saddle. I stayed 13 years on one ranch and earned $7.50 a month." He said that after three to four months, his wages were raised to $12.50 per month. The years brought more responsibility, and he was hired by "a man from Boston, who leased the ranch and turned it over to me." Mills continued, "I done all the hirin' and payin' off and buyin' and 'everthing'." The ranch was eventually sold, and Mills began leasing other ranches and making their cattle business profitable.

The average Texas ranch had 8 cowhands, usually 4 Black men and an equal number of white men. In Indian Territory, all the cowhands were often Black. The XIT Ranch was huge, the largest ranch in Texas, covering 3 million acres. It had a payroll of about 150 cowboys, at least half of whom were Black. The ranch was divided into eight divisions; each had a foreman, 8 to 20 cowboys, a cook, and a remuda of 100 horses or more. There were 150,000 longhorns and 1,000 horses on the ranch, and there were several cattle drives annually. Starting in 1889, the XIT cowboys drove about 12,500 head one thousand miles to leased grasslands in Montana every year.

The cattle grazed for one to two years to build up weight before they were shipped to market.

Cowboys needed horses to get their work done, and mustangs were invaluable. They were descended from horses brought to the Americas by Spanish explorers in the 1500s. These wild horses were valued for their incredible stamina, endurance, and exceptional intelligence, which made them great cow ponies. Mustangs could turn on a dime, flash into top speed, and vanish, and only a skillful mustanger could capture them.

Robert Lemmons was a mustanger who lived and breathed mustangs and became a legend in his time. He was born enslaved in Texas, was emancipated at seventeen, and took his boss Duncan Lemmons's last name. He herded cattle, but his real interest was in wild horses, which he studied and developed a unique way of capturing. Working alone, isolated from other people, he gained a mustang herd's trust, infiltrated it, and then took control of it. No other mustanger ever achieved his level of skill or his ability to actually lead herds of wild horses into ranches, just like the Pied Piper of mustangs.

Mustangs made good cow ponies once they were trained. Breaking and training them was a challenge and required time and patience. Bones Hooks, Jim Perry, and Jim Kelly built outstanding reputations as riders, able to manage and train these wild horses. Black bronc busters were often hired by ranchers to break and train their horses and were paid between three and five dollars per horse. Youthful Black bronc busters earned about twenty-five to fifty cents for each horse they broke.

The workday on the ranch began in the early morning when the wrangler brought the remuda in and put the horses in the corral. Some horses, despite their training, usually started the day by bucking, snorting, and getting the kinks out before they settled down. After years of breaking and training mustangs, Jim Perry had a knack with them, and he could "stick to a horse's back like a lean tick to a dog's ear."

Every ranch had at least one outlaw horse, and at the XIT, it was a beautiful bay with wicked ways called Rosy Brown. Only Jim Perry could ride her. One XIT veteran recalled, "Every mornin' the horses were brought into the corral, and you'd see some poor boy shakin' in his boots, standin' there after everyone else is mounted. Rosy Brown is still waitin', an evil gleam in her eye." Jim would ask the boy quietly, "Want me to top her for you?" The youngster would nod and grin gratefully, and Jim would swing into the saddle and quickly take the starch out of Rosy. Cowboy W.T. Brown said, "Not only was Jim the best cook but the best Negro that ever lived, as

Jim Perry playing the fiddle. He was a top-hand bronc buster and a renowned chuck wagon cook. *Public domain.*

well as the strongest and best rider.... If they [the broncos] threw me, he would always ride them for me."

Jim Perry was a top hand and all-around cowboy at the XIT Ranch for more than twenty years. He was born in Texas in 1858 and was working on a ranch by the time he was a teenager in 1870. After several years on the range, Jim began cooking and driving the chuck wagon on trail drives. He was a culinary genius, and his contemporaries said he was the best cook to ever work on the XIT. When he wasn't driving the chuck wagon, he drove freight wagons, delivering windmill parts, feed, and supplies to scattered XIT districts.

Jim was a talented fiddle player, and his ballads and trail songs around the campfire turned cowboys' thoughts to home. He often played lively jigs and rollicking reels for dances and celebrations at the ranch.

There wasn't much upward mobility for a Black cowboy, despite his ability. Jim Perry earned the respect of his white contemporaries, but his opportunities for advancement at XIT were limited by his skin color. Although he could have handled the responsibilities, and despite his long relationship with the ranch manager and the XIT, Jim was never promoted to foreman or trail boss. Occasionally, he'd ruefully say, "If it wasn't for my damned old black face, I'd have been boss of one of these divisions long ago."

When Jim was fifty in 1917, he married Emma Beasley, who could read and write and helped with operations at the XIT headquarters. Tragically, he developed a brain tumor when he was sixty and underwent surgery, but he did not survive the procedure. Jim Perry died on August 2, and hundreds of friends gathered for his funeral. He was buried at the white cemetery in Channing, Texas, the only Black person to be allowed burial there. Bert Meade, a Panhandle resident, wrote, "The only Negro cowboy in the Tascosa-Channing area known to current residents and the only Negro was buried in this cemetery, known just as 'Jim' to his contemporaries, but so well liked by all that there was no dissent in burying him in a white cemetery as one might expect at that time."

Horses were an important part of the cattle business, and without horses, cowboys and ranchers couldn't operate. There were four jobs for a horse on a ranch or trail drive: roping, cutting, riding, and standing night guard. Specialized training was necessary to produce a good cutting horse. A cutting horse and his rider worked together to separate a single animal from a herd of cattle and keep it from getting back to the herd. If a cowboy started after an animal, and the cutting horse identified it, the horse would take off after it himself, slowly haze it out of the herd, and prevent it from escaping. A cutting horse often worked only two to three hours and was replaced by another for the rest of the day.

A roping horse watched the cowboy's rope and stopped the instant he saw that he'd caught the animal. As the cowboy ran to tie a steer's legs, the horse pulled the rope taut so the animal couldn't get up. This was hard on a horse's hooves and front legs, and he often developed soreness behind his shoulders from the strain.

A strong horse that wasn't good at cutting out steers would be used for daily ranch work, roundups, and trail drives. These horses usually worked four to five hours in the morning, and the cowboy switched horses for the afternoon. A top cow horse was gentle and very surefooted, careful to avoid falling. He had a good sense of direction and awareness of his location. If a cowboy became lost miles from camp in the dark, a good cow horse could usually find his way back home.

Ike Ward was once enslaved and became well known as the best roper around Beeville, Texas. In his book *Texas Cowboy*, Charlie Siringo wrote that he'd partnered with Ward when cowboys were road branding a herd before a trail drive. This is wild and wooly work, and a good roper is important. The team of Ward and Siringo worked well together, and Charlie said, "By the end of the night, Old Ike was bragging about his great new partner to the other cowboys."

Black cowboy Frank's quick thinking and skill with the lariat once saved Ab Blocker's life. A visitor to his camp recalled the event. He said that the outfit was "nooning," and Frank, known for his roping skills as "Blocker's roper," had just ridden into camp, dismounted, and dropped the reins, ground tying his horse. He was going to get a cup of coffee when Ab Blocker started yelling for help. Frank looked up and saw Ab running with a big steer right behind him. Frank threw down his cup, ran to his horse, tossed the reins over the horse's head, and jumped into the saddle. He twirled his lasso and raced toward the steer as the charging animal lowered his head, ready to hook Ab. Frank rode up, whirled the lasso around his head, and hollered,

"Hold on Boss don't go no further!" Then he threw the lasso over the steer's horns. The beef whipped around and changed ends as the horse pulled the rope tight. That steer was so close to Ab that he was almost touching his back when Frank flipped him off his feet, stopping his deadly charge!

Roundups were held every spring and fall to gather calves for branding and separate steers for market. A cow camp was set up with a chuck wagon, and the cowboys remained there until the roundup was finished. When there were no fences to confine cattle, they roamed for miles, and cowboys worked together to find them. After the cattle were in pens, they were sorted by their brands and earmarks by a "rep" from each ranch.

Upset cows were held in pens while their bawling calves were branded, earmarked, and castrated. A large fire was built to heat as many as fifteen different branding irons at one time. The ropers often worked in pairs, with one man who roped the front legs of the animal, tipping him over, and then the other who stretched him out and held him down until the outfit's brand was seared into his hide and the earmarking and castration were done. The brand and earmark of each rancher were registered with the county clerk, and theft of cattle with registered brands was prosecuted.

After the roundup, every spring cowboys from the XIT Ranch moved cattle from the Panhandle to Montana on the Great Western Trail, which had several branches running through northeastern Colorado to Wyoming, Montana, and Dakota. The XIT often had several herds of two thousand head each on the trails at the same time, and these spring drives took four to five months. The longhorns traveled ten to fifteen miles per day, and the cowboys endured severe storms, floods, and stampedes. The climate on the northern plains was very different from Texas, and storms in early summer often brought wet, heavy snow. Later drives in the summer were hit by sudden snowstorms in August and early September. After the cattle were delivered in Montana, most cowboys were glad to leave the cold and snow and return to the warmer Texas weather.

In the 1880s, railroads expanded into Texas and Montana, bringing shipping depots closer to these cattle pastures. Once trains were available, the XIT shipped its cattle and cowboys north from Texas to Wyoming, unloaded the herds there, and drove them east to Montana. After the herds were in the pastures, the cowboys rode their horses back to the train in Wyoming, loaded their horses, and returned to Texas in comfort. Only a few Black cowboys stayed in Montana, and most, like Big Gus, found work in saloons, restaurants, or hotels.

Cowboys branding cattle on the XIT Ranch. *Library of Congress.*

George Fletcher wearing Angora chaps at Pendleton Round-Up, circa 1911. *W.S. Bowman, Oregon Historical Society Research Library, 67878.*

Big Gus was a "big dusky man" who'd cooked on many trail drives before leaving the XIT Ranch. In 1895, when he was head cook at the Windsor Hotel in Sheridan, Wyoming, he had a big wood pile behind the hotel. If a hobo asked for a free meal, Gus told him how to earn it and sent him out to the wood pile. Some men took off their coats, checked the axe blade for sharpness, and got to work. Others were disgusted and just walked away, looking for an easier handout.

Bob Leavitt drove thousands of cattle on the Great Western Trail to Montana with XIT crews in the 1880s. He'd been a cook at a ranch division in Texas before he decided not to return. Bob liked Montana and was hired by the N Bar N Ranch, where he worked for years. In 1895, at a large combined roundup with the XIT, Bob was a respected "rep" for the N Bar N. He sorted hundreds of calves and got them branded, earmarked, and sent back to the home range. Harry Longbaugh broke mustangs at this Montana ranch before he became the Sundance Kid and joined Butch Cassidy robbing trains and banks.

One soggy morning during fall roundup, when it was so rainy that little work could be done, the cowboys spent the day riding unruly broncs. Somebody managed to get the cook, Bob Leavitt, on a horse, certain that he'd quickly be tossed into the mud. J.A. Smiley, another ranch cowboy, laughed and said, "It kept us guessin' who would win—Old Bob or the bronc. Finally, the bronc lost, but Old Bob had just about give it up when the bronc finally gave out!" Leavitt worked with young greenhorn Charles Russell, who launched his career as a cowboy artist at the N Bar N Ranch. After several years, Bob had saved enough of his earnings, quit cowboying, and bought a saloon in Miles City, Montana. Old photographs show him standing proudly in front of "Bob's Saloon."

Big Joe liked to play rousing tunes on his banjo in the XIT bunkhouse, but his real fame came from his enormous feet. Big Joe had the biggest feet any cowboy had ever laid eyes on, and he insisted on walking around without shoes. Big Joe spent the entire summer barefoot and even rode his horse without boots! Despite their lack of a formal education, some Black cowboys who couldn't read or write overcame this challenge and through hard work and determination carved out a place for themselves in the cattle business. Black cowboy Thornton Biggs and Texan Hiram "Hi" Bernard were hired to turn a failing ranch into a successful cattle business by New Englander Ora Haley, who wasn't making any money on his Two Bar Ranch in Wyoming. Both men knew cattle, and their employment freed Haley to pursue his political interests and win election to Congress.

When Wyoming was granted statehood, Haley served in the first Wyoming state senate in 1890.

Meantime, Bernard and Biggs managed Haley's ranch well, importing white faced Herefords to improve and strengthen the longhorn breed and purchasing hay pastures in northern Colorado to raise feed. The cowboy and foreman developed the Two Bar into the largest ranch with the most cattle in Wyoming and western Colorado.

In 1903, Hi Bernard married Anne Bassett, the "Outlaw Queen," who'd been rustling Haley's cattle on the side. The rancher was furious and fired Hi, leaving Thornton Biggs to run the ranch. More land was acquired, and the herds grew as Biggs continued his wise operation of the Two Bar. Newspaper articles and a report published in the *Negro Cowboys* by Phillip Durham and Everett Jones credited Ora Haley's phenomenal success in the cattle business to "the contribution made by a long-time employee, a colored man named Thornton Biggs, the best top hand to ever fork a bronc or doctor a sick cow on the Laramie Plains." The report continued, "Although he never became a range manager or even a foreman, Biggs taught a whole generation of future range managers, wagon bosses, and all-around cowpunchers the finer points of the range cattle business." Haley eventually sold the ranch and retired in Denver, while Biggs worked on a ranch near Laramie until he died in 1941.

Another success story belongs to cattle rancher C.F. Cox and cowboy George Adams, who developed a mutual trust and worked together to build two successful businesses. Little was known about George Adams when he was hired at C.F. Cox's 7D Ranch around 1902. He was a top hand, an expert with the lariat, and had driven cattle on the Goodnight-Loving and Chisholm Trails. He was excellent with horses and had trained them for the Second Cavalry in Texas. Since there were two Georges at the ranch, Adams was called "7D George" or simply "George." He worked at the Cox ranch for thirty-eight years, and when his wages were due, Cox often said, "Go brand a cow. You've earned it." When Cox decided to raise sheep instead of cattle, he asked George to be his partner and take over the cattle business.

The two men became close friends, and George taught Cox's two grandsons how to rope and ride, as well as all about the cattle business. Adams was always included in family celebrations and important events. During the Depression, sheep prices were low, and Cox was unable to make his mortgage payments. He was in danger of foreclosure and losing the ranch, so George Adams put up his herd of cattle as collateral. The bank renewed his loan, and Cox kept his ranch.

George never learned to write or read, but he spoke English well and was fluent in Spanish. He preferred a simple life, lived in the bunkhouse, and managed the cattle. Once a year, he led the local rodeo parade and always supplied the cattle for the rodeo's roping events. He died at ninety-five in September 1939, two years after Cox. Before his death, Cox extracted a promise from his family that when his old friend and partner George Adams died, he would be buried beside him. The family agreed, but their promise created an uproar among the town's citizens and the Cox family. Since maintaining segregation, even in death, was so important in Texas, the Cox family broke their deathbed promise to their father and buried his best friend and partner George Adams at his feet.

A TRUSTED FRIEND AND RIGHT-HAND MAN

These accounts are about close friendships and deep trust that developed between a Black employee and his white employer. Confidences were kept, advice was given, and wisdom was shared. As loyalty was proven, trust was built and friendship developed. The Black men in these accounts were trusted with financial information, gave advice about business transactions, and knew personal secrets. For their fidelity, they received fidelity in turn, as well as friendship and respect.

SHANGHAI PIERCE AND NEPTUNE HOLMES

In December 1853, Abel "Shanghai" Pierce, a New England Yankee, strode down the gangplank of a ship on the East Texas coast with seventy-five cents in his pocket and a big dream. He was going to become a "millionaire Texas cattleman." Since he needed money to buy cattle, he got a job splitting wood for Bing Grimes, a wealthy rancher. The tall, lanky, six-foot-four young man was nicknamed Shanghai because he reminded others of a banty Shanghai rooster with his long, skinny legs and pants that were too short. Throw in the musical jingle of shiny spurs and the cocky strut of a self-made dynamo and you have Abel Shanghai Pierce. He would become one of Texas's most colorful, loud, rascally cattle barons in just a few years. Bigger than life, Shanghai cut a wide swath wherever he went, and always at his side was his most trusted confidant and friend, a Black man named Neptune Holmes.

Shanghai quickly surpassed his humble beginnings swinging an axe and advanced to handyman status, patching Bing Grimes's roof and mending his fences. One spring morning in 1854, the corral was full of wild, ornery mustangs to be broken and trained for the cowboys to ride. As fast as the bronc busting crew got a saddle cinched on the back of a snorting mustang, Bing shoved one of his slaves forward to climb aboard. The group of Black men clustered around the corral cheered their fellow on as the mustang rolled and pitched and tried his best to send his unwelcome rider into the sky. The reluctant bronc busters had varying degrees of success, but many were bucked off. Then a particularly fractious stallion was brought out, wild-eyed and snapping his teeth. Suddenly, Mrs. Grimes's shrill voice yelled from the ranch house, "Bing! Those Negroes are worth a thousand dollars apiece! One might get killed! Put Abel on those bad 'uns!"

The unwilling bronc busters laughed hilariously as Shanghai Pierce, the handyman, gave Grimes a withering stare and yelled loud enough to be heard inside the house, "All right, bring on your bad 'uns!" Then he stepped boldly forward to face the wild stallion that had just unloaded another rider. He climbed aboard and yelled, "Let 'er rip!" The horse reared wildly and vaulted upward, mane flying and hooves flailing. Coming down with a thud, he took short, stiff crow hops around the corral and then gathered himself, arched his back, and sprang up with all four feet off the ground. He bucked, twisted, sun-fished, and turned his belly toward the sky while Shanghai hung on, glued to the saddle. Returning to earth, the exhausted stallion, breathing heavily, stood head bowed, his quivering flanks heaving and frothy with sweat. There were loud cheers for the handyman as Bing announced that Shanghai was promoted to the ranch's bronc buster.

Shanghai wanted his wages paid in cattle, but after Bing cheated him with a few worn-out old cows, the future millionaire demanded cash and bought livestock himself. Shanghai's brother, Jonathan, joined him, but the Civil War interrupted the Pierce cattle enterprise; despite being Yankees, both brothers joined the Texas Cavalry. When Shanghai left for his stint on the Rebel forces, Grimes owed him $500 in wages, which he was assured he'd be paid when he returned.

When the war ended, Grimes paid Shanghai in worthless Confederate money. The furious Pierce brothers quit on the spot, and Shanghai swore that he would get even, promising to send Grimes to "the Black Hills," symbolizing a financial graveyard. By 1866, the Pierce brothers had established their Rancho Grande, and by 1871, they had more than 100,000 head of cattle roaming over fifty square miles of land. As the Union Pacific advanced west, Shanghai drove his cattle to the closest rail head and then used profits from sales to buy more land. By 1872, he owned more than 500,000 acres, including the land where Bing Grimes grazed his cattle. Then, through a series of financial maneuvers, he had the satisfaction of putting Bing out of the cattle business and sending him to "the Black Hills."

There were more than fifty cowboys working for Shanghai and Jonathan at the Rancho Grande, and several were Black, including Ben Kinchlow, Charlie Ellis, brothers Robert and John Norman, Ed Roberts, Jasper Singleton, G.W. Carson, Ed Partain, and Clay McSparrow. Gabriel Simms loved playing poker and was always ready for a game with the boys. The most picturesque ranch hand was Podo, a very tall, dignified Zulu from South Africa who went about his tasks quietly, carrying a wooden staff that was taller than he was. Podo finally gave up his native costume of just a leather breechclout and agreed to wear short pants.

By 1870, Neptune Holmes, once a slave, had become Shanghai's most trusted friend, always accompanying him on cattle buying trips, carrying the money, and wearing his six-shooter. On more than one occasion, loud, boisterous Shanghai took Napoleon's shrewd, quietly offered business advice. The two men conducted transactions side by side, every day, for more than thirty-five years. Where you found Shanghai, you'd find Neptune.

Shanghai understood why Texas cattlemen wanted "hard money" for their cattle. Marvin Hunter, who compiled *The Trail Drivers of Texas*, described one of Shanghai's cattle buying trips: "He [Pierce] was a large portly man who always rode a fine horse and would be accompanied by a Negro, Neptune, who led a pack horse loaded with gold and silver. The money was dumped on a blanket and remained there until the cattle were counted out. Then he would pay it out to the different stockmen from whom he purchased. He would generally buy two or three hundred head at a time…we all looked at him as a redeemer, a gift from heaven because money was scarce in those Reconstruction days."

When Shanghai was around, his booming voice could be heard for half a mile, even when he tried to whisper. He knew everyone and always yelled out greetings. When a friend was asked if Shanghai was in town, he replied, "No, I haven't seen him, but I know he's not here because I haven't heard him!" In 1896, Shanghai and Neptune spent sixteen days traveling from town to town buying gold to pay off bank notes. Shanghai went into the bank to conduct his business while Neptune waited outside in the street with the horses and a pack mule loaded with gold. Neptune was well armed, and no one ever tried to rob them.

Black cowboys. *Black Past, Black Cowboys in the 19th Century West (1850–1900).*

Both men married and raised families, and Neptune built a comfortable house on seventy-seven acres of land near Pierce Station. He refused additional gifts of land from Shanghai, saying that he had enough. Neptune saved money to be certain there was enough to take care of his family and ensured that his nine children graduated from a school for Black children. When Shanghai was getting on in years, he commissioned a sculptor to create a marble statue of himself that was to "be higher than any statue of any Confederate general." When the statue was finished, he wouldn't pay the sculptor until Neptune approved his work. After inspecting the statue, Neptune reported, "It looks just like you Mr. Shang." Then Shanghai wrote out the check.

Shanghai Pierce died in 1900 and was buried at the cemetery where his marble statue marks his grave. Neptune grieved for his friend and remained at the ranch, making his rounds on horseback with his six-shooter strapped around his waist until he was eighty. He developed pneumonia and died at eighty-two in February 1934. Hundreds of Black, white and Hispanic friends shed tears at Neptune's large funeral, for he was everyone's friend.

Print Olive and Jim Kelly

Jim Kelly, the child of former slaves, grew up on a Texas ranch with Jim Olive's four sons, where he was treated as an equal and felt no shame in being Black. He ignored neighboring ranchers who weren't wealthy enough to own slaves but who shared the racist attitude of many southerners toward Black people and called him insulting names. He learned to rope, ride, and shoot with the Olive boys and formed a close bond with Print Olive. He went to West Texas during the late 1850s to avoid the increased talk of secession and the growing hostility toward "freed Blacks." He returned when the war was over to help the Olive brothers build their cattle business.

The Olive men rounded up wild longhorns, while Jim Kelly broke and trained mustangs for the ranch's cowboys. As they acquired more land, settlers learned quickly that Olive territory was off-limits. Jim was an expert with the six-shooter, rifle, and shotgun and became the top enforcer for the clan. When rustling threatened to wipe out their herd, Print Olive and Jim Kelly took the law into their own hands and shot the cattle thieves. Print developed a deadly reputation, and few dared cross him or risk his anger. He was always armed, quick to shoot, and usually accompanied by the formidable Jim Kelly. If suspicious strangers were encountered around the Olive cattle, they used their six-shooters first and asked questions later.

Under Kelly's direction, all cowhands wore guns and knew how to use them. Cowboy E.C. Abbott, "Teddy Blue," who worked for the Olives and later wrote about his cowboy life in *We Headed Them North*, described them as a "gun outfit." He said that the Olive brothers were "violent and overbearing" and that they all had "black eyes just like a rattlesnake's and a temper to match." He said the Olives hated Mexicans and "Blacks, although they hired plenty of them," adding, "It takes a hard man to work for them and believe me they had plenty."

In March 1872, Print, Kelly, and a crew including Black cowboy Henry Strain Jr. and several *vaqueros* drove a large herd of steers to Ellsworth, Kansas. Print sold the cattle for twenty-five dollars per head, and he and his friend Gene Lyons went in search of a friendly poker game. Their game became unfriendly when Print accused another player, Jim Kennedy, of cheating. The card player denied it but angrily threatened Print and stomped out.

Print and the others continued gambling at a table near the front of the saloon, which had large glass windows. Chairs were lined up outside so citizens could observe the activity inside as well as on Main Street. Jim Kelly and the *vaquero*, Alberto, were strolling down the wooden sidewalk when they saw Print and Lyons playing poker through the saloon's window and sat down outside to watch.

The accused cheater, Kennedy, returned to the saloon and suddenly shot the unarmed Print, hitting him in the hand and twice in the thigh. Outside the saloon, Jim Kelly, who wasn't aware of their quarrel, heard the shots and quickly turned his head. He saw Print lying on the floor, with Kennedy standing directly over him, firing down. Kelly whipped out his six-shooter and, in one movement, whirled and fired through the window, never leaving his chair. The slug caught Kennedy in the hip with such force it knocked him off balance, and as Lyons punched him in the head, he toppled to the floor.

Kelly ran into the saloon, picked up Print, and set him on a table, while someone hurried for the doctor. Kennedy was held for the sheriff. Two physicians rushed into the saloon, managed to slow the bleeding from Print's wounds, and then carried him to their office. A third surgeon removed the bullets and a portion of Print's gold watch chain that had been driven into his thigh. The remainder would be removed by a Denver surgeon months later.

Print hovered between life and death for a week in a hotel room with Jim Kelly by his side. Gene Lyons hid the gold from the cattle sales under the chuck wagon's false bottom and took the trail crew and horses back to Texas. When Print was strong enough to travel, he and Kelly returned home on the train. Print's wounds healed slowly while the 1873 financial crisis wiped out cattlemen and left him with few assets.

Throughout 1875–76, Print and Kelly fought rustlers stealing their few cattle, and both were arrested but acquitted for the torture-murder of two thieves. The rustlers banded together in a large gang, far outnumbering the cattlemen, and threatened to overrun the county; the *Austin Statesman* newspaper reported that twenty-one men were murdered in the county. Print sent his brother, Bob, and Jim Kelly to Kansas, Nebraska, and Colorado to locate suitable grasslands that would support their cattle. When the pair stopped in a small Nebraska town, Jim went into the saloon to buy whiskey for Bob. When he asked the proprietor for a bottle of bourbon, he was ignored, while other customers muttered about "colored cowpunchers." Kelly got the bartender's attention when he put his hand on his big revolver and growled, "I came here to buy a bottle of whiskey—not be made the fool by a bartender...pass me a quart of that bourbon and I'll be peacefully on my way." There was dead silence until the proprietor, a red-faced Irishman, handed a bottle to the gunman. Kelly paid and left, overhearing a Texas cowboy warn, "That's Jim Kelly, Print Olive's bad gunslinger. You'd be smart to leave him alone."

The Olives decided to leave Texas to start a new ranch on thousands of acres of grassland that Kelly and Bob Olive had located in Nebraska. They drove their herds north, rebuilt, and soon had the largest cattle ranch in Nebraska. Unfortunately, homesteaders had discovered this area, too, and once again there was trouble. Jim Kelly as the Olive enforcer drove longhorns into the farmers' fields, cutting barbed wire fences, burning crops, and terrorizing the "sodbusters." Rustlers stole the Olive cattle and killed Bob Olive. When two of the rustlers were captured, Print and a posse lynched them, but Print lived to regret taking the law into his own hands. When the two dead rustlers were hanging from the branch of an elm tree, someone threw whiskey on their bodies and ignited them. Print was blamed and called "Man Burner." When a gruesome photo of the two burned corpses appeared in the newspapers, everyone was horrified and turned against him.

Print Olive, Jim Kelly, and members of the posse were arrested and tried for manslaughter. Kelly and the men who didn't take part in the lynching were released and their charges dismissed. In 1879, Print was convicted of second-degree manslaughter and spent a year in prison waiting for his appeal to be heard. There was a second trial, but since none of the original witnesses appeared, the charges were dismissed. There were rumors that Print spent all his money on legal fees and bribes to secure his release, and by 1880, he was overwhelmed with debts. He sold the Nebraska ranch and went to Dodge City with Jim Kelly. There he bought a saloon in Trail City on the Colorado-Kansas border. He loaned money to a man named Joe Sparrow, who was gradually repaying this debt. On August 18, 1886, when Print impatiently pressed him to make the final payment of ten dollars, Sparrow shot and killed him.

Jim Kelly disappeared, but the last years of his life were spent in Ansley, Nebraska. He died in February 1912 and was buried at the town cemetery. His grave is marked with a monument engraved "James Kelly Died Feb. 7, 1912 Legendary Figure of Custer County."

John Chisum and Frank Chisum

John Chisum was one of the first Texas cattlemen to drive a herd west to New Mexico on the Goodnight-Loving Trail. Chisum's name is often confused with that of Jesse Chisholm, an Indian trader, whose wagon route from Texas to Kansas was named after him. John Chisum sold beef to the Confederacy, but unlike his acquaintances, Charles Goodnight and Oliver Loving and others who were paid in Confederate dollars, he lost little money from these deals.

After Goodnight and Loving's lucrative cattle sales at Fort Sumner in 1866, Chisum saw an opportunity and took a herd of nine hundred cattle over that trail in August 1866. Most of his cowboys were experienced hands, except for his young wrangler, Benjamin Franklin Chisum, a Black boy about seven or eight years old, who was purchased when he was four with another boy, Thomas Jefferson Chisum. Both boys became part of the household, and young Frank slept on the foot of Chisum's bed to keep his feet warm. Frank had a knack with horses and cattle, and at eight, he became the wrangler on Chisum's cattle drives.

Chisum formed a partnership with Charles Goodnight after Oliver Loving died, and he drove 10,000 longhorns annually to Bosque Grande for the following three years. Goodnight developed new markets and handled the sales and delivery of the Chisum cattle to the army and ranchers in Colorado and Wyoming. Using money from these cattle sales, Chisum established a ranch at Bosque Grande in 1872, claiming rangeland extending 150 miles down the Pecos River. He built a huge empire of more than 100,000 cattle and adopted the Long Rail brand and the Jinglebob earmark. This distinctive mark was a lateral slash through the middle of the animal's ear, leaving the lower half dangling beside the head.

Portrait of John Simpson Chisum, famous cattle king, from *The Story of the Outlaw* by Emerson Hough, 1907. *Amon Carter Museum of American Art, Fort Worth, Texas.*

Frank Chisum, trusted friend and right-hand man to cattle baron John Simpson Chisum. *University of New Mexico Digital Repository.*

Frank Chisum was devoted to John Chisum, lived at the ranch, and was always included on trail drives. As he grew older, he became Chisum's trusted friend and right-hand man. He had an uncanny knack with horses and often was able to detect illness or injury in an animal and manage its treatment. He could handle unruly horses and was able to train and transform a feared outlaw into a willing saddle horse. Frank was unanimously praised by all who knew him as "the best line rider and horseman" they'd ever seen.

By 1882, John Chisum had moved ten miles down the valley near Roswell and built a rambling ranch house on South Spring Creek. Although he never married, his home was always full of family and friends, and his niece Sallie managed the household. In 1884, John developed a malignant tumor on his neck that was removed in Kansas City. Then he went to Eureka Hot Springs, Arkansas, hoping that the mineral baths would help him recuperate, but his condition worsened. John Chisum died three days before Christmas 1884; he was sixty years old.

Historian Mary Whatley Clarke wrote in a biography of Chisum, *John Simpson Chisum, Jinglebob King of the Pecos*, that when his niece Sallie needed money to operate the ranch, "Frank, faithful as always and loving the Chisum heirs as his own family, financed Sallie." This helped her keep the ranch together for several years after Chisum's death.

Over the years, Frank had often asked to be paid his wages in cattle, and he'd gradually accumulated a small herd with his VF brand. After John Chisum died, Frank refused an offer from the Chisum heirs to combine his herd with theirs in a business enterprise. When their venture failed, Frank still had his cattle, and his herd had increased considerably in size. He remained in the Roswell area, and the *Las Vegas Optic* noted on August 26, 1885, that "Frank Chisum is in the city today. He is a colored man and has gone into the cattle business for himself by gradually working into it. His bunch of cows now numbers 125 head, and he is as proud of them as the greatest king on the plains." Bob Boze Bell wrote in *True West* of October 2020 that "in the teens and early twenties, Frank is noted in the 'old-timer' parades as having worked for many other 'large cow outfits in eastern New Mexico, serving with the Blocks, Bar Vs, Circle Diamonds, Diamond AZ, Flying HS, and others.'" The January 10, 1929 *Amarillo Daily News* reported, "At old-timer reunions he was always placed at the head of the parades where he could be seen riding the finest horses the country afforded and dressed in the uniform of a Confederate officer, a relic sent to him from the Southland and one of his most prized possessions.

Chisum Ranch, Roswell New Mexico, from *The Story of the Outlaw* by Emerson Hough, 1907. *Public domain.*

Chisum Ranch (South Spring Ranch), Roswell, New Mexico postcard. Cowboys are ready for the roundup. *University of North Texas.*

At the barbecues, Frank was always given a place of honor, serving the pioneers in the same fashion which for more than a half century he served the cow outfits."

Mary Clarke wrote in her biography of John Chisum that Frank had a dream in which John Chisum sent him the message, "We want you." Frank told his friends in Roswell that that he was going back home to die and to be buried near his master, John Chisum. He died in Texas in March 1929 at age seventy-three.

John Slaughter and John Hinnaut, John Swain and Jim Young

Everyone knew him as "Old Bat," since his proper name of John Battavia Hinnaut was quite fancy for an enslaved man. Born in 1841 in the South, after emancipation he was hired as a cook for the Slaughter brothers' trail drives. When John Slaughter moved his entire herd from Texas to Roswell, New Mexico, Old Bat was on the drive and remained at the new ranch. When Slaughter decided that southern Arizona was a better location for his cattle business, Old Bat helped move the cattle operation and eventually became Slaughter's trusted right-hand man.

When the rancher traveled about Arizona buying cattle, he always wore a money belt filled with $10,000 in gold. Old Bat accompanied him as his bodyguard, armed with a rifle and six-shooter. To avoid an ambush by Apaches or bandits, Slaughter always took a different route on these business trips. Bat was in charge of the mule loaded with Mexican pesos hidden beneath the bedrolls and provisions. Despite these precautions, Slaughter and three trusted cowboys once were attacked by a large gang of Mexican bandits when they entered a canyon near the border. With bullets whizzing around their heads, Slaughter and his companions dived behind huge boulders along the canyon wall and returned the gunfire. After several hours, they finally drove the Mexicans off, turned around quickly, and made it safely back to the ranch.

Slaughter was always too busy to worry about his own health, so Old Bat did it for him. He reminded "Uncle John" to wear a coat when it was cold, to forego sweets, and to eat plenty of fruit instead. He urged Slaughter to eat proper meals and take care of his teeth. Old Bat brushed his own teeth every day, and his toothbrush was always sticking out of his shirt pocket. Slaughter was fond of Old Bat and often showed his appreciation for his

"Texas" John Horton Slaughter (1841–1922), American lawman, Arizona cattleman, Civil War soldier, and gambler. *Amon Carter Museum of American Art, Fort Worth, Texas.*

"nurse's" caregiving with cases of soft drinks. This was Old Bat's favorite treat, and he guarded it carefully, right down to the last bottle.

Old Bat loved music and was often heard tootling away on his squeaky old fife. He was quite proud when he was the first person in Tombstone to buy the newly invented gramophone. He carefully placed his precious treasure, with its shiny brass morning glory horn, beside him on the wagon seat and took it everywhere he went. When he traveled to Sonora, Mexico, with John Slaughter, he played some lively tunes for bystanders and laughed heartily when a little boy tried to crawl into the gramophone's horn "to see where the music came from."

Five years after the Gunfight at the O.K. Corral, Slaughter was elected sheriff of Cochise County and began his battle against outlaws and Apaches. He had the help of John Swain, known as Sweeney, who was an excellent tracker, able to follow any trail in the rocky desert. The Black man was invaluable when he joined Slaughter, army troopers, and settlers in pursuit of Geronimo and his band in the 1880s. Sweeney was born enslaved in 1845 in Texas and given to the Slaughter family when he was a young boy. As a cowboy on Slaughter's Texas ranch, he drove cattle to New Mexico and Arizona.

Once Slaughter, Sweeney, and Old Bat tracked a herd of stolen cattle driven into Mexico by rustlers. They crossed the border, surprised the outlaws, killed a few, and drove the rest away. Then they began driving the cattle back toward the Arizona border, but the surviving rustlers pursued them. Slaughter spotted a box canyon, and they quickly drove the cattle in and took up protected positions near the entrance. The Mexicans charged the canyon, but Bat and Sweeney, who were both expert shots, began picking them off. Then Sweeney emerged from cover and boldly advanced through the mouth of the canyon, firing his shotgun. These deadly blasts scattered the rustlers, who quickly whirled about and rode off. When the coast was clear, Slaughter and the three cowboys emerged from the canyon and drove their recovered cattle back to the ranch with no more trouble.

As he grew older, John Slaughter continued to operate his cattle business with the help of Sweeney and Old Bat. They remained on the

John Swain Slaughter was a Black cowboy who spent his life as a trusted employee and friend of Arizona rancher and lawman "Texas" John Horton Slaughter. *Public domain.*

ranch for years until Slaughter finally decided to move to town. He died on February 15, 1922, in Douglas, Arizona. Little is known about Old Bat after Slaughter died, but Sweeney moved to Tombstone, where he lived in a little cottage behind the Cochise County Courthouse. He was nearly one hundred when he died in February 1945. The March 2 *Apache Sentinel* wrote, "Tombstone's Oldest Citizen, Ex-Slave Fills Last Grave in Town's Boot Hill. Fort Huachucans Pay Respect to Deceased Pioneer. Independent until his last days; Mr. Swain kept his little cottage behind the Court House spotlessly clean; he tended his own garden plot; and he walked pridefully about the streets of Tombstone as he had walked about those streets in the halcyon days of the 80s. So independent was he that he had even put aside $100 of his own small pension money to provide for his burial. It is at his own request that his remains are buried in Boot Hill, near those whom he had known during the early days when he was one of the hardest riding cowboys in the region."

Jim Young, another cowboy who was with Slaughter for several years, was born in Texas and emancipated. After the Civil War, he joined the Buffalo Soldiers and fought Indians in Texas with the Ninth Cavalry. When he was discharged from the army, he was hired by Slaughter for cattle drives to New Mexico. He made the move to Arizona and worked on Slaughter's ranch until he got the mining bug. When silver was discovered near Tombstone, Jim quit cowboying, got a job in a mine, and filed his own mining claim.

When Buckskin Frank Leslie, a notorious Tombstone killer, tried to jump Jim's claim, the Black man grabbed his shotgun and ran him off. Jim was a giant of a man with tremendous strength and the courage to back up his actions, so Leslie moved on to easier prey. When news of the conflict between the disliked outlaw and the Black man went around Tombstone, Jim received plenty of praise and pats on the back.

Jim had some experience boxing, and after winning several bouts with other miners, he had a stellar reputation. In 1884, John L. Sullivan, the first world heavyweight boxing champion, came to Tombstone on a coast-to-coast tour with five other boxers. Everyone wanted to see the champ and crowded around a boxing ring that was set up on a stage at Schiefflin Hall. John L. created a lot of excitement when he offered to fight the four biggest men in Tombstone, all in one ring and all at the same time! No one accepted

that challenge, so the champ bragged that he could knock out a mule with one punch. Again, no one was willing to put up their expensive mule on a bet. Since he still didn't have an opponent, John L. challenged the crowd with an offer to pay $500 to any man who could go four rounds with him and still remain standing after the final bell. Jim quickly raised his hand, and the match was set.

The rowdy bunch of prospectors, cowboys, and miners, well fortified with alcohol, swarmed around the ring, while gamblers rushed about taking bets. Excitement grew in the smoky hall as Jim stripped off his shirt, donned his boxing gloves, climbed into the ring, and waved to the crowd. John L., dubbed the "Boston Strong Boy" by the press, flexed his impressive muscles and smirked. When the opening bell rang, both men quickly moved into the center of the ring. Jim, who was well over six feet tall, towered over the much shorter, muscular

Jim Young in Tombstone, Arizona, July 1927. He was a cowboy at the John Slaughter Ranch. At ninety-four, he remained an imposing figure. *Arizona Historical Society Library & Archives.*

champion. The crowd cheered, whistled, and stamped its feet when Jim let fly with a looping roundhouse that caught Sullivan on the forehead and sent him staggering into the ropes. The miners cheered, but the champ quickly recovered, feinted with his left, and then his right delivered a whopping clout to Jim's jaw, knocking him flat. The crowd groaned while their hero was stretched out on the canvas, unconscious for fifteen minutes. Total time of the bout: six seconds.

Finally, Jim was lifted over the ropes and carried out of the hall feet first. When the champ issued another challenge, no one stepped forward. Disgusted, the hard-hitting, hard-drinking Sullivan celebrated his victory at as many of Tombstone's 110 saloons that he could stagger into. The next day, the bout was reported in the *Tombstone Epitaph*, which colorfully described Sullivan dropping the Black boxer "like a ton of coal." When Jim was interviewed by reporters, he complained that he "felt dopey" and wondered if he'd been doped!

Jim Young remained in Tombstone for more than fifty years. As one of the few remaining residents from the town's wildest days, he rode in the first Helldorado Days parade, which was celebrated in October 1929. Jim Young died on January 19, 1935, in Tucson and was buried there.

SUCCESS STORIES

Some Black cowboys weren't content to simply care for another man's horses, herd another man's cattle, dig another man's postholes, or live in another man's bunkhouse. They didn't want to occupy a piece of earth that belonged to someone else. They wanted their own land, their own cattle, and their own house. They knew that they had to work twice as hard and be much better than others to overcome the prejudice of the day. They dreamed, planned, and worked hard to succeed.

GEORGE MCJUNKIN

George McJunkin was born enslaved in Texas around 1856 and learned to ride and speak Spanish from Mexican *vaqueros*. He left home at seventeen and was hired as a wrangler on a cattle drive to Abilene, Kansas. When they reached the railhead, George spent his wages on a bath, haircut, new clothes, a saddle and rifle, and a fine horse, which he rode proudly back to Texas. Next he was hired by mustangers, who were rounding up wild horses to sell in New Mexico and Colorado. They'd captured about seven hundred horses and were headed west on the Goodnight-Loving Trail when they stopped to hunt more. Their herd was confined in a box canyon, and George was left to guard them. Unfortunately, a band of Comanches swooped down and stampeded the herd, and as the mustangs raced out

George McJunkin, circa 1907, cowboy and amateur archaeologist who discovered the Folsom site. *Public domain.*

of the canyon, McJunkin's horse broke loose and joined them, taking his new saddle and rifle with them. George raced for cover as the screaming Indians charged after him, arrows flying wildly. When the Comanches realized that he was unarmed, they started laughing loudly, waved their rifles over their heads, and rode off with the mustangs.

A few days later, the mustangers returned after capturing only a few horses and learned that their entire herd had been stolen by the Comanches. They weren't angry at George but were disgusted that they'd have to catch hundreds of horses again. George borrowed a horse, and the crew got busy. They rounded up several hundred mustangs, drove them to New Mexico, sold them, and took Goodnight's route north across Trinchera Pass east of Trinidad, Colorado. Gideon Roberts, a mustanger, decided to start a horse ranch here on the Purgatory River near the Mountain Branch of the Santa Fe Trail. He hired George to break and train mustangs into good saddle horses, which soon brought high prices.

Ranch supplies were purchased in Trinidad, and on one trip George bought a violin, which he taught himself to play. Once he had mastered this musical instrument, he occasionally visited the little settlement of Trinchera, where he met other musicians and played for the settlers in the Plaza. Gideon Roberts's sons taught George to read and write, and he showed them how to break and train horses. George developed an interest in history and spent his free time roaming the prairie, collecting arrowheads, bones, and artifacts.

After a few years with Roberts, George was offered a job by Dr. Thomas Owen, a partner in the large 101 Ranch in northern New Mexico. He was placed in charge of a crew to build a house and barn for a new ranch in the Cimarron Valley. Although Dr. Owen had fought for the Confederacy, he hadn't been a slave owner, and he treated George with respect and began teaching him about running a ranch. As time passed, George was included in special Owen celebrations and was treated like a member of the family. He ate with them in the ranch kitchen and taught the doctor's sons, Ben and Tom, how to ride and take care of horses and cattle.

Dr. Owens made George foreman of the Cimarron Valley ranch and a second new one, the Pitchfork Ranch, fifty miles away. He was responsible for more than two thousand head of cattle, two hundred horses, and twenty cowboys. At first, the white cowboys resented taking orders from a Black man, but after they worked with George and saw his ability roping, riding, and handling livestock, their complaining stopped.

The winter of 1889 was hard on New Mexican ranchers, and Dr. Owen lost almost 1,500 head of cattle and most of his horses in several weeks of snowstorms and frigid temperatures. George and fourteen cowboys were caught in a blizzard on the open range, but he managed to get everyone safely to a remote line cabin. They waited out the storm there, thankful for the shelter and a warm fire in the woodstove.

In 1891, Dr. Owen, his good friend and mentor, became ill and died suddenly, leaving George to look out for Mrs. Owens and her two young sons. Now thirty-nine years old, George took over running the two ranches, helping her raise the boys and teaching them how to manage the business. After several years, when the boys were older, George turned over the ranch management to them and took a job as foreman of Bill Jack's eight-thousand-acre Crowfoot Ranch.

Once again, George was in charge of all aspects of the ranch's cattle business, and he was treated like a member of the Jack family. He lived in the ranch house, and Mrs. Jack gave him a set of encyclopedias and books on astronomy, fossils, geology, and early dinosaur discoveries. George was an avid reader with an insatiable curiosity and studied in his free time. He was interested in astronomy, and as an amateur archaeologist, he was proud of his large collection of bones, fossils, rocks, and artifacts.

George dreamed of owning a piece of land with a house and a herd of cattle bearing his three-quarter circle brand. The Jacks encouraged him, and he started saving his wages to buy land in the Cimarron Valley. George was the only Black person in this part of New Mexico and at times endured discrimination, but he was widely respected and had many friends. However, there were no Black women around, and his hopes of marriage were fading. There were some available Hispanic women, but Hispanic men strongly discouraged his association with them. Bowing to public pressure, George was still a bachelor at forty.

On August 27, 1908, a severe thunderstorm dropped fourteen inches of rain on the region, and the sudden flood destroyed buildings and damaged the town of Folsom. George rode around the huge Crowfoot Ranch, assessing the damage. In Wild Horse Arroyo, floodwaters had washed a gully ten feet deep. He saw a huge bone protruding from the side of the wash, buried several feet deep. George grabbed a shovel and started digging, and after several hours of work, he excavated the large bone. Amazed at its size, he was certain that this bone was from some long-extinct animal.

George contacted numerous museums and universities about his discovery, but no one was interested. He unearthed more bones in the "Bone Pit," and in 1912, he met Carl Schwachheim, who was interested and promised to visit. Time passed and Carl didn't come. A few years after his discovery, George told Fred Howarth, a Raton banker, about the Bone Pit, but once again, a visit never materialized.

Despite George's many letters to scientific institutions, his discovery was still ignored. Then his friend Mr. Jack died, leaving George once again in charge of a ranch. Now sixty-five years old, he decided against buying the property himself, and it was eventually sold. Unfortunately, George's home near Folsom was struck by lightning, and the fire destroyed the house, his fossil collections, and his treasured books. Depressed by this huge loss and his failing health, George moved into the Folsom Hotel, where he could get his meals. Many young cowboys he'd taught to rope and ride visited, brightening his days with their stories. Old-timers came to share memories and reminisce about the past.

George's health grew worse, and he died on January 21, 1922, at the hotel. There was a large funeral attended by his numerous friends and cowboys he'd taught, and he was buried at the Folsom Cemetery. He was seventy-one years old.

Ironically, several months after George died, Carl Schwachheim and Fred Howarth belatedly came to see the Bone Pit. They brought two other men, and they dug up more bones and took them to Raton. These bones sat in boxes for four years until 1926, when Howarth and Schwachheim took them to the Colorado Museum of Natural History (now the Museum of Nature and Science) in Denver. The director, Dr. Figgins, a paleontologist, was very interested and soon visited the Bone Pit himself. He recognized the significance of George's findings and ordered the scientific excavation of the Pit.

At least thirty extinct bison skeletons were unearthed, but the most exciting discovery was a spear point found embedded between a Pleistocene bison's ribs. Two spears with fluted, man-made points were also turned up and authenticated by scientific authorities, placing early man in the Southwest more than ten thousand years ago. George McJunkin's Bone Pit, renamed the "Folsom Site," proved that Ice Age hunters had crossed the Bering Strait centuries earlier than scientists first believed. This set off a huge wave of interest in archaeology in the Southwest.

Schwachheim and Howarth unashamedly took all the credit for the discovery of the Bone Pit, and McJunkin's name wasn't mentioned in any scientific publication. Then, in 1972, almost fifty years after George died, Paleo-Indian archaeologist George Agogino of Eastern New Mexico University heard stories about McJunkin from people living in the Folsom area. He and writer Franklin Folsom tracked down and recorded stories from people who knew George and about his initial discovery of the Bone Pit. They documented his role in this important event, finally giving George the credit he was due.

NAT LOVE

Deadwood Dick! Nat Love earned his nickname fair and square because he was the best roper, the best rider, and the best shot in Deadwood, South Dakota. On July 4, 1876, our nation's one hundredth birthday, before his own twenty-first birthday, Nat Love outshot, outroped, and outrode a bunch of wild cowboys in Deadwood and won $200 and a nickname that stuck with him for life. Nat lived the rough-and-tumble cowboy life, and his exploits made him one of the most famous heroes of the Old West. His story was so exciting that he decided to share it with others, and in 1907 he published his memoirs, *The Life and Adventures of Nat Love, Better Known in the Cattle Country as Deadwood Dick*.

Nat Love, a Black cowboy nicknamed "Deadwood Dick" in South Dakota, 1876, was known for his roping talent. *From his privately published autobiography (1907), via Wikimedia Commons.*

Nat was born enslaved in a Tennessee log cabin in 1854, and his father taught him to read and write. After emancipation, his father died, leaving Nat to support his family by working in the fields and doing odd jobs until he began breaking horses for ten cents each. He mastered most animals easily until he was challenged by a fierce black stallion with an uncertain temper and wild disposition. This job was surely worth fifty cents, but Nat compromised for twenty-five cents, paid in advance. The stallion took him on a wild ride, jumping fences, bucking and racing through pastures, stampeding the other horses, and riling up the dogs in the neighborhood, but Nat managed to stay in the saddle. Unfortunately, he lost his quarter while doing it.

Nat's chance to see the world came with a raffle ticket that he bought for fifty cents and won a fine horse, the first prize. This was such a great horse that the owner knew he could make more money by raffling him off again, so he talked Nat into selling the animal back to him for $50. Flush with cash, Nat bought another fifty-cent raffle ticket and once more won the horse. Again, he sold the horse back to the owner, collected another easy $50, and headed home with $100 in his pocket. Nat gave half the money to his mother, left her in the care of his uncle, and at fifteen years of age headed for Kansas to become a cowboy.

In Dodge City, Nat met several Black cowboys from the Duval Ranch in Texas who'd just finished a cattle drive. He asked the trail boss for a job, but since he was a greenhorn, he had to prove his mettle by riding Good Eye, the meanest horse in their outfit. When he climbed into the outlaw's saddle, he held on tight as the bucking, rearing, jumping bronc did his best to toss him skyward. He said, "I thought I had ridden pitching horses before, but from the moment I mounted Good Eye I knew I had not learned what pitching was. This proved the worst horse to ride I ever mounted in my life, but I stayed with him, and the cowboys were the most surprised outfit you ever saw!" Nat got the job at thirty dollars per month and rode off to Texas to begin his career as a cowboy.

After three years in the Panhandle, Nat was a skilled roper and rider, and he'd sharpened his shooting skills holding off Indians and rustlers and bringing down buffalos and bandits. He spoke Spanish fluently, which was helpful when he and the boys went to Mexico to bring back a herd of horses. On one return trip, Nat developed a mighty thirst, and since he didn't want to bother dismounting, he rode his horse right into a saloon, scattering the crowd around the bar with a few well-placed bullets. He ordered tequila for himself and pulque for his horse from the surly bartender. When an angry crowd gathered outside the saloon, Nat realized that they meant business: "I put my spurs to my horse, dashed out of the saloon, knocking over Mexicans right and left." He raced off in a hail of bullets and made straight for the Rio Grande.

In 1872, Nat Love left Texas for Arizona and was hired at the Gallinger Ranch on the Gila River. He became Pete Gallinger's right-hand man and drove herds to scattered shipping points, all while fighting off rustlers. He was wounded and captured by Indians, and when his injuries healed, he was expected to marry the chief's daughter. Anxious to remain a bachelor, Nat escaped that trap and made it back to the ranch.

On July 3, 1876, Nat and the Gallinger cowboys drove three thousand longhorns into Deadwood Gulch, South Dakota, after following the Goodnight-Loving Trail through New Mexico and Colorado to Cheyenne and Dakota. This large, well-armed crew of cowboys had just learned that General Custer and the Seventh Cavalry had lost a big battle with Indians a few days before.

After selling the cattle, Nat and his friends were off to celebrate Independence Day in Deadwood. The citizens had organized a contest for cowboys, who'd come from miles around, and they'd raised a purse of $200 for the winner of a challenging roping contest. Twelve of the most vicious mustangs were chosen from a wild herd, and a horse was selected for each contestant, six of whom, including Nat, were Black. Each cowboy was to rope, tie, bridle, saddle, and mount his mustang in the shortest time possible. The one who got it done the fastest was the winner.

With the crack of the revolver, everyone jumped to their mustang. Nat roped and saddled his mount in nine minutes, while his closest competitor needed twelve minutes. Nat won the contest and was named the "Champion of the West." He held that title until 1890, when he retired from the cowboy life, and his record was never beaten. Years later, recalling that competition, Nat said that he'd "never had a horse pitch with me as much as that mustang!" He stuck on the bronc through its bone-breaking leaps and jumps and proved to be its master.

Next came the shooting competition to determine who was the best shot with a Colt .45 and a rifle. Nat was competing against some of the top guns in the West: Powderhorn Bill, Stormy Jim, and a "halfbreed" known as Whitehead, plus several others who could handle a gun. Each contestant had fourteen shots with the rifle and twelve with the Colt. The shooting began, and Nat placed all fourteen of his rifle shots in the bull's-eye; then, shooting the Colt from the hip, he put ten shots in the center ring, outshooting all the others. Nat was the champion, winning the roping contest and the shooting contests, and the cheering crowd proclaimed him "Deadwood Dick," a name he would carry with honor the rest of his days.

The Deadwood champion spent several days celebrating his new title before hitting the trail back to Arizona. Nat remained with Pete Gallinger for years and had plenty of hair-raising adventures and narrow escapes, and he survived being shot fourteen times "in fourteen different places." He met some heroes and several shady characters as he traveled about the West. Bat Masterson bought him a drink, and he shared a whiskey or two with Billy the Kid. He befriended outlaws Frank and Jessie James and met Pat Garrett and showman Buffalo Bill Cody.

As the years went by, Nat saw changes in the West. Barbed wire and settlers took over the open range, and cattle traveled on trains, not trails. He traded his cowboy duds for a new blue uniform with shiny brass buttons and gave up his cow pony to ride an iron horse. He went to work for the Pullman Company as a porter in the luxury cars of the Denver and Rio Grande Railroad, married, and moved to Denver.

In 1905, Nat pulled up stakes, and the *Salt Lake City Tribune* announced his plans: "Colored Porter as Author—Nat Love or Deadwood Dick Will Tell His Experiences." Nat's book about his wild life was published in 1907 and received a lot of attention. It was as thrilling as any dime novel and had as much excitement as his life. Nate wrote, "Mounted on my favorite horse, my...lariat near my hand, and my trusty guns in my belt...I felt I could defy the world." And he did.

BONES HOOKS

Matthew Hooks was born in Texas in 1867, the child of slaves who'd taken the last name of their owner. After emancipation, the Hooks moved to a nearby town, where Matthew's father became a minister, taught other Black people to read, and instilled in his son a sense of community responsibility. Since he could read and hitch a mule team when he was seven, Matthew was hired to drive the butcher's wagon around town, and at nine he was driving it on out-of-town trips.

Matthew was thin and wiry, with long legs, earning his nickname of "Bones." Cowboys taught him to ride, but Bones observed, "They made me the best bronc rider in the country, but they weren't really trying to make me a rider. They were trying to get me throwed!" Sometimes the cowboys put him on a horse bareback or without a bridle. Bones remembered, "They put me on a big gray horse and turned him out of the corral, him pitching and running, and me without a bridle or anyway to hold or guide him." Somehow he managed to stay on the horse for twelve miles until the cowboys chased him down. With experiences like this, he quickly learned to stick on a horse's back like a tick. By the time he was fourteen, Bones was working as a wrangler, earning twenty-five dollars per month and busting broncs for three to five dollars per horse.

In the 1880s, Bones broke horses for Charles Goodnight, who'd returned to Texas with sixteen thousand longhorns to start his JA Ranch in the Panhandle. By 1887, Bones was working with hundreds of mustangs at the huge XIT Ranch. He avoided the rowdy

Matthew "Bones" Hooks was a cowboy, horse breaker, and trainer in the Panhandle. He developed a small community for Black citizens near Amarillo, built the first church for Blacks, was active in community, and held many charitable activities. *Panhandle-Plains Historical Museum, Canyon, Texas.*

towns near the ranch headquarters, hoping to settle down in Clarendon, which was founded as a "Christian town" by a Methodist minister. Unfortunately, this Christian town did not accept Black Christians. Matthew was told plainly, "Negroes are not allowed in this town!" Determined to win acceptance, Bones quietly made friends around the community and trained horses for local ranchers. Although Bones was eventually acknowledged, it was years before he was allowed to buy a small piece of land and build a house in Clarendon.

There was plenty of work for Bones in the Panhandle until the disastrous winter of 1885–86 killed thousands of cattle, bankrupted ranchers, and forced many to leave. Blizzards were followed by a severe drought that dried up the grass and streams and killed off the few surviving cattle. Bones moved to northeast Texas and bought a small grocery store near Texarkana. One morning, he found a sign tacked to the door, "We give you 36 hours to get out," signed by the "White Caps of Sand Gall Gizzard." Bones closed his store and left town immediately. He returned to Clarendon, but the cattle business had declined—farmers had planted crops where cattle once grazed. Many towns still refused to accept Black

Black cowboys at the Negro State Fair. Bonham, Texas, circa 1913. *Public domain.*

people, and some wouldn't even permit a Black traveler a brief rest stop. The 1880 Panhandle census listed fifty-seven Blacks, and several of them were working cowboys.

In 1894, the Clarendon town fathers permitted Bones to buy a small lot where he built a church for Blacks; it was one of the first African American churches in West Texas. He imported a preacher from Fort Worth, and Black families were finally allowed to make their homes in Clarendon. Bones started a horse breaking business with a close friend, Tommy Clayton, a white cowboy. They prospered until tragedy struck when Tommy's horse fell on him, killing him. At Tommy's funeral, the grieving Bones placed a bouquet of Tommy's favorite white wildflowers on his coffin. As a memorial to his friend, he began sending white flowers to the funerals of Clarendon pioneers and gradually expanded this tribute to people who had made notable contributions to the community. Bones continued this practice the rest of his life.

In the waning days of the nineteenth century, there wasn't much demand for a cowboy who could break horses, so Bones moved to Amarillo, becoming the town's second Black resident. Segregation was the norm, so he decided to establish a new, separate community for Black people nearby and convinced his friend, the mayor, to help finance the initial effort. The new hamlet of North Heights grew quickly, and Bones invested every penny he'd saved to build a combination drugstore/general store there.

Bones married, worked ten years as a porter in an Amarillo hotel, and was hired by the Pullman Company, which managed the elegant sleeping cars on the Santa Fe Railroad. One day in 1910, when he was forty-three years old, he overheard a group of ranchers talking about an outlaw horse that no one had been able to ride in Pampa, Texas. Bones interrupted, saying, "I can ride that horse!" Everyone scoffed until he bet twenty-five dollars (most of his salary) on himself. The contest was quickly arranged, and two days later, the train stopped at the Pampa depot and passengers hurried off to see the show. The white-jacketed porters gathered together to cheer for Bones, and a large crowd of people came out from town. Bones smiled at the eager spectators, took off his porter's cap and jacket, and slipped on his cowboy boots as the snorting, wild-eyed outlaw was led out. There was no corral, but Bones quickly climbed into the saddle. The bronc took off, jumping straight up, sun-fishing, twisting, and turning wildly in the air. Bones stuck with him, riding that one thousand pounds of dynamite to a quivering standstill. The crowd cheered and clapped, and the passengers who were hanging out of the train windows waved their scarves and hats. Bones stepped up and collected his winnings and then donned his jacket and cap, gave a wave to the crowd, and boarded the train. This feat made Bones famous, and the story stuck with him the remainder of his time with the Pullman Company. He retired in 1930 after more than twenty years with the railroad.

Black boys could not join Amarillo's youth organization, the Maverick Club, so Bones organized the Dogie Club for poor, fatherless boys so they could camp and play organized sports. He became the first Black person in Amarillo to serve on a county grand jury and continued sending white flowers to pioneer families and people who'd made notable achievements. For years,

Matthew "Bones" Hooks, cowboy and trailblazer. *Public domain*.

143

he'd saved newspaper articles about Panhandle pioneers in scrapbooks, and his large collection was included in a national exhibit in Detroit titled "75 Years of Negro Progress."

In 1932, Bones and members of the Black community dedicated a new park with a lovely fountain and trees that were planted by the town's children. Each tree was named after someone living in North Heights. A year after the park opened, the town fathers named it in honor of Bones Hooks, who had established this vibrant community. Bones died in 1951 at age eighty-three, and several years later, the townspeople gathered in the park to dedicate a bronze statue of the community-minded cowboy. Every year on Juneteenth, June 19, there's a celebration with a barbecue, baseball game, and speeches in Bones Hooks Memorial Park. Bones Hooks was inducted into the National Cowboy Western Heritage Museum Hall of Fame during the 2021 National Western Heritage Awards in Oklahoma City.

JOHN WARE

Imagine having a postage stamp issued in your honor! John Ware was honored this way when Canada issued such a commemorative stamp during Black History Month in 2012. It was designed with a photograph of Ware and a drawing of a bucking horse as a tribute to the Black rancher and in recognition of his national historic significance in Canada.

After the end of the Civil War, John Ware, a Texas cowboy, joined trail crews driving cattle to New Mexico on the Goodnight-Loving Trail and the Chisholm Trail to Abilene and Dodge City. In the 1870s, he went north on the Great Western Trail to Montana, and in 1882, he was in a crew that drove three thousand head to Sir Hugh Allan's North-West Cattle Company in Alberta, Canada. Allen and a British syndicate started the new Bar U ranch, which covered 160,000 acres near Calgary. John decided to stay in Canada and was hired by the Bar U, which soon had thirty thousand cattle and one thousand Percheron horses.

Ware worked with Harry Longbaugh, who was breaking horses at the Bar U. This was before Harry took up a new career as an outlaw, the Sundance Kid, riding with Butch Cassidy. There were very few Black cowboys in Canada, and Ware became well known for his ability to ride any bucking horse. In 1884, Ware was hired by a syndicate forming the new Quorn Ranch on the Sheep River in Alberta. The owners imported twelve Thoroughbred stallions from England, and one named Eaglesplume became famous in

John Ware was born enslaved. He became a cowboy, and during a cattle drive to Canada, he decided to remain. He began ranching in Alberta in 1887. He was a folk hero and was honored with commemorative postage stamp in 2012. He's pictured with his wife, Mildred, and two of their six children. *Public domain.*

western Thoroughbred racing and horse breeding lore. John Ware was placed in charge of this expensive herd because of his knowledge and ability to manage horses.

Ware was well liked and received a lot of publicity in the Canadian press. The *Macleod Gazette* of June 23, 1885, proclaimed, "John is not only one of the best natured and most obliging fellows in the country, but he is one of the shrewdest cow men, and the man is considered pretty lucky who has him to look after his interest. The horse is not running on the prairie which John cannot ride." The Quorn Ranch expanded and imported 1,500 head of cattle from Montana in 1885, but the blizzards, deep snow, and frigid weather in the winter of 1886–87 wiped out most of the herd. The ranch faced bankruptcy but was finally able to obtain a loan and continue operations until 1906.

Over the years, John Ware became a folk hero in Canada, and the stories of his feats as a cowboy were legendary: he could stop a steer racing headlong toward him and wrestle it to the ground, and he could ride the most notorious, wildest bronc. There were even tales that he could easily lift an eighteen-month-old steer and toss it on its back for branding. It was said that he was strong enough to hold a horse down on its back while the farrier put on horseshoes. He was often credited for introducing bulldogging, later called steer wrestling, at the Calgary Rodeo. Despite his popularity, Ware encountered racial prejudice and was often referred to as the "Negro Cowboy."

John saved his wages and bought land and some cattle, realizing his dream of having his own ranch in the Alberta foothills near the Sheep River. He built a log cabin and married, and he and his wife had six children. By 1887, Ware owned two hundred head of cattle and had registered his brand of four 9999s, which was called "the walking stick" brand.

The Ware family moved to the Red Deer Valley near Duchess, Alberta, in 1902. John was the first to develop an irrigation system to water his crops of oats, barley, and vegetables. His herd had grown to about one thousand cattle when his home was destroyed in a spring flood. Ware built a larger house on higher ground, but in the spring of 1905, his wife, Mildred, developed pneumonia and died. Just a few months later, in September 1905, there was another tragedy when John's horse stepped in a badger hole and fell on him. John's neck was broken, and he died instantly.

Alberta's citizens were shocked by the sad news that John Ware had died in such a tragic accident, and his young children were now orphans. Ware's funeral was one of the largest ever held in Calgary, and it was attended by hundreds of people. John had many friends, and they came from miles around to pay tribute to a man they respected and admired. John Ware was buried at Union Cemetery, overlooking the Calgary Stampede Rodeo Ground, and his orphaned children were taken in and raised by their grandparents. During World War I, two of the Ware sons, Arthur and William, joined the No. 2 Construction Battalion, the only all-Black battalion in Canadian military history.

In southern Alberta, John Ware's memory and name live on in numerous geographic landmarks, like Mount Ware, Ware Creek, and John Ware Ridge.

John Ware with his dog in Alberta, circa 1891. *Glenbow Museum Archives, Calgary, Alberta, Canada.*

In 1958, the log cabin John built for his family was relocated from its prairie location to the Red Deer Valley, restored, and placed at Dinosaur Provincial Park, where it was rededicated in 2002.

Calgary is home to John Ware Junior High School, and at the Alberta Institute of Technology, the John Ware Building houses the 4 Nines Dining

Center. Youngsters have hands-on learning experiences in the John Ware 4-H Beef Club in Duchess, Alberta. Diamond Joe White, an Alberta musician, wrote a song titled "High Rider: The John Ware Story." In 2012, during Black History Month, a commemorative stamp honoring John Ware was issued. In 2022, the Canadian government designated John Ware as "a person of historical significance."

DANIEL WEBSTER WALLACE

Picking cotton for thirty cents per day was a hard way to support yourself. After emancipation, Daniel Webster Wallace left home at fifteen years of age to become a cowboy and was hired as a wrangler on a cattle drive. When the drive reached the Kansas railroad, the cattle were sold, and Daniel was paid his wages of fifteen silver dollars.

He learned to break mustangs and refined his roping skills, and when his cowboy friends challenged him to rope a buffalo, he did it not once but twice. When he was seventeen years old, he was hired by rancher John Nunn, who branded his cattle with a large "80" burned into the animal's hide from "backbone to belly" to thwart rustlers. When Daniel drove herds to the railhead, folks began calling him "80 John," associating him with Nunn's ranch.

The 1870s were a dangerous time in Texas, with the Comanches rampaging, always lurking in the brush, eager to steal cattle and snatch white men's scalps. John became good with a revolver and rifle and moved on to a better opportunity with wealthy rancher Clay Mann. He began to learn the business of ranching from Mann, who owned cattle and vast amounts of land in Texas, New Mexico, and Chihuahua, Mexico. The rancher taught him about buying cattle and improving the herd, as well as the importance of acquiring good range land for grazing.

When he was asked to handle a task, Wallace always replied, "I will do my best." The two men developed a close, trusting relationship, and as Mann's right-hand man, he often traveled miles from ranch headquarters to buy and sell cattle, scout rangeland and trails, and evaluate new opportunities for expansion of the business. To complete purchases, Mann often entrusted Wallace with large sums of money. Once on a three-day journey, Wallace used the bag containing the $30,000 down payment for a land purchase as his pillow. His skin color wasn't a hindrance as he conducted business with cattlemen, investors, and bankers.

After getting a herd to market, Wallace negotiated a fair price for the cattle and collected payment in gold. Wallace always put his wages aside and didn't join the cowboys in gambling or drinking, explaining that he was saving his money to buy his own cattle ranch. He was well liked by the men and respected for his fairness and willingness to carry more than his load. When he was in his mid-twenties, Wallace asked Mann to withhold money from his wages every month, and he used these

Daniel Webster "80 John" Wallace was born enslaved in 1860. He worked as a cowboy and saved his wages for years to buy cattle and land. He became a respected member of the Texas ranching community. His ranch is in operation today. *Public domain.*

wages to buy land and build his own herd. By the time he was twenty-five, Wallace owned two sections of land and had homesteaded each. Acutely aware that he could not read or write, the six-foot-tall cowboy enrolled in the second grade with local children. He married the teacher in 1888 and settled down on his land.

Wallace was devastated in 1889 when Clay Mann, his friend and mentor, died. He continued managing the ranch and Mann's holdings for the next two years while training the rancher's two sons to run their father's business. After they took over, Wallace worked for wages to get his own ranch established and to make ends meet. He loaded cattle into railroad cars to be shipped to market and worked as a cowboy for local ranchers. He leased some of his own acreage to other farmers and borrowed money to buy Durham cattle to improve his herd. He set aside acreage and planted supplemental feed crops for his cattle.

Over time, through hard work and careful planning, Daniel Wallace became a very successful, respected cattle rancher. He had a large crew of Black and white cowboys and paid them well. Wallace survived the Great Depression and bought additional land, which increased his ranch size to 8,820 acres. Daniel Wallace eventually became a millionaire and was always very generous, donating money for churches and to build schools for Black children. He was a member of the Texas and Southwestern Cattle Raisers Association for thirty years and owned sixteen properties, including his 10,272-acre Silver Creek Ranch. When Daniel "80 John" Webster Wallace died in March 1939, he left an estate worth more than

$1 million. He was buried on his ranch, which is still owned by his family. A state historical marker in Loraine, Texas, commemorates his life, and a school was named in his honor.

ADDISON JONES

Imagine receiving nineteen cookstoves on your wedding day! When fifty-four-year-old bachelor cowboy Addison Jones got married on Christmas Day 1899, his numerous friends did their best to give the newlyweds a special wedding gift. When Mr. and Mrs. Jones were summoned to the Roswell Freight Depot to pick up some recently delivered shipments, they were surprised to see that nineteen cast-iron cooking stoves from the new Montgomery Ward catalogue had been sent by well-wishers!

Old Ad was a top hand at George Littlefield's LFD Ranch and spent his entire working life helping the rancher manage his enterprises. Littlefield started his cattle business in 1871 when he gathered a herd and drove it to Abilene, Kansas, where he sold it for enough money to pay off his debts and start a business. He began buying and selling cattle, and after making one trail drive, Littlefield realized that he had other talents and delegated the responsibility of running a drive to experienced trail bosses. He turned his attention to building cattle herds and brokering their sales. Once he'd purchased a herd, he arranged its sale and a trail drive to deliver it to the buyer. He had several herds on the trail at the same time, and in 1877, he moved twenty-three thousand cattle.

Old Ad made many drives on the Goodnight-Loving and Chisholm Trails for George Littlefield. There were always Black cowboys in his trail crews, and Black cowhands worked year-round on Littlefield's ranches in Texas and New Mexico. Slaves had always been part of Littlefield's life, and he recognized their skill with cattle and horses. There was Old Cuff, a veteran of the Goodnight-Loving Trail; "Big Wash" Littlefield; another hand known simply as "Lasses"; and Aleck Stewart. Curly the Crow, who claimed he was a Crow Indian, despite his kinky hair, was cook for Littlefield outfits. The cowboys tolerated his tall tales about scouting for Custer because he baked delicious peach pies in the Dutch oven and whipped up desserts of creamy rice and raisins.

The boys were always glad when a big Black man known to most as Sam joined their crew as cook. He turned out sourdough biscuits light as a feather, and his cheerful disposition and talent with the fiddle made him one of the most sought-after cooks in Texas. Littlefield had no trouble keeping trail drivers and crews because of his reputation for fairness and paying high wages.

It's not known how Ad Jones and George Littlefield became acquainted, but they were about the same age and were closely associated most of Ad's life. Jones always had more responsibility than the other cowboys, and sometimes he worked on a distant part of the ranch in charge of a large crew of Black cowboys. He often accompanied Littlefield on cattle buying trips and supervised drives to railheads. In addition to his astute business sense, Ad was a top cowboy who excelling in roping, bronc riding, and managing cattle on the trail.

Ad Jones was a short but powerfully built man, able to combine his strength and agility with skill and a knowledge of horse nature. It was said that he could "read a horse's mind by staring it in the eye." Trail boss Phelps White recalled, "He could walk into a corral full of broncs, and he had such a powerful grip that he'd get one by the ear and nose with his bare hands, smooth him down, and lead him out of the bunch." There were plenty of stories reflecting Ad's rare ability to reassure a wild bronco and earn the animal's respect.

Texas cowboy, circa 1910. He's seen here holding a rope around the neck of a bucking bronco on a ranch in Texas. *Library of Congress via Amon Carter Museum, Erwin E. Smith Collection.*

Deputy U.S. Marshal Robert Fortune, *far right*, is seen circa 1900 in Indian Territory during a search for fugitives. Fortune became a civil rights attorney in Oklahoma and Arizona. Amos Maytubby is on the left, with Deputy Marshals Zeke Miller and Neely Factor. *Western History Collections, University of Oklahoma Library*.

Ad was well known for his skill at breaking broncs, and on a trail drive, he often "topped off" several horses every morning to get the pitching out of their systems. In the cold predawn hours, while the other cowboys were finishing breakfast, the wrangler brought the saddled horses into camp, backs humped, eyes rolling, ready to resist. Climbing on one of these bad-tempered mustangs was a punishing, bone-jarring way to start the day. A cowboy like Ad Jones, willing and capable of taking that first pitch out of these rough horses, was greatly appreciated by the crew. Most cowboys who were in their thirties were reluctant to face this challenge because their bodies just couldn't take it anymore.

When Ad worked at spring roundup, cowboys were relieved because he would ride horses that everyone else feared. Ad's string of mounts was always made up of the worst horses in the outfit, and it wasn't unusual for even his night horse to come unwound when he saddled up. Flying into a wall-eyed fit, the bronc would pitch and jump right through the middle of the camp, scattering Cookie's pots and pans and galvanizing sleepy-eyed cowboys. Fellow cowboy J.D. Hart said that Addison Jones rode as if he'd been born to ride horses: "Ad kicked the living daylights out of those jug-headed horses that didn't know when to stop."

Jones was also known for his precision with a lasso. J. Evetts Haley, a historian, described a roping technique Addison used in *Black Cowboys of Texas*: "He tied a rope around his hips, then roped the horse around the neck, and as he raced past at full speed Ad would, by sheer will and power on the end of the rope, invariably flatten the horse out on the ground!" Haley noted that anyone else would have been dragged to death. Old Ad was known far and wide and became a legend around Texas and in the New Mexico Territory.

Ad didn't have much education and was barely able to read or write, but he was an encyclopedia of cattle brands and earmarks. In 1889, Howard "Jack" Thorp, a cowboy who collected and published the first booklet of cowboy ballads, camped with Ad and marveled at his ability to quickly identify different brands and earmarks. Thorp even wrote a song about Ad and his encyclopedic knowledge of brands called "Whose Old Cow?"

Ad worked at the LFD Ranch for many years and finally retired with his wife, Rosa, in Roswell, where he owned his own home. He was a familiar, popular face around town and was a member of the Knights of Pythias and a Mason. In a world where cowboys were mostly anonymous ranch hands, Addison Jones became a legend, and he was mentioned in numerous memoirs written by prominent cattlemen and local cowboys who'd worked with him. He was eighty-one when he died on March 24, 1926. Rosa died just a few years later, and both are buried in South Park Cemetery in Roswell, New Mexico.

Bass Reeves, the first Black U.S. deputy marshal. He captured more than three thousand criminals in Indian Territory. *Western History Collections, University of Oklahoma Library.*

The era of the great cattle drives only lasted about twenty years, and by the late 1890s, barbed wire fencing was enclosing the Great Plains. The Homestead Act of 1862 had drawn settlers west with the promise of free land. Now farmers planted their crops where longhorns once grazed, and the railroad followed the old cattle trails. The open range was no more. An old cowboy fondly recalled his time on the trail when he said, "I rode the range when it was new, before barbed wire fences. We ate; we slept; we rounded up longhorns; we branded them; we marked their ears; and we drove cattle as free and happy as if we were on a lark." Life on the range and ranch brought less discrimination to Black cowboys, and their world expanded, offering new opportunities.

BIBLIOGRAPHY

Abbott, Edward (Teddy Blue), and Helen B. Smith. *We Pointed Them North: Recollections of a Cowpuncher*. New York: Farrar &Rinehart, 1939.

Adams, Andy. *The Log of a Cowboy*. Boston: Houghton Mifflin Company, 1903.

Adams, Ramon. *Come an' Git It: The Story of the Old Cowboy Cook*. Norman: University of Oklahoma Press, 1972.

Anschutz, Philip. *Out Where the West Begins*. Denver, CO: Cloud Camp Press, 2015.

Atherton, Lewis. *The Cattle Kings*. Bloomington: Indiana University Press, 1961.

Bard, Floyd. *Horse Wrangler: Sixty Years in the Saddle in Wyoming and Montana*. Norman: University of Oklahoma Press, 1960.

Billington, Monroe Lee, and Roger Hardaway. *African Americans of the Western Frontier*. Niwot: University Press of Colorado, 1998.

Branch, Hettye Wallace. *The Story of "80 John": A Biography of One of the Most Respected Negro Ranchmen in the Old West*. New York: Greenwich Book Publishers, 1967.

Brayer, Garnet, and Herbert O. Brayer. *American Cattle Trails, 1540–1900*. Denver, CO: Smith Brothers. Printing, 1952.

Broussard, Albert. *Expectations of Equality: A History of Black Westerners*. Wheeling, IL: Harlan Davidson, 2012.

Brown, Dee. *The American West*. New York: Simon & Schuster, 1994.

———. *Trail Driving Days*. New York: Charles Scribner's Sons, 1952.

Burton, Art. *Black, Red, and Deadly: Black and Indian Gunfighters of the Indian Territories*. Austin, TX: Eakin Press, 1991.

Caldwell, Clifford. *John Simpson Chisum*. Santa Fe, NM: Sunstone Press, 2010.

Carlson, Paul, ed. *The Cowboy Way*. Lubbock: Texas Tech Press. 2000.

Chisholm, Joseph. *Brewery Gulch: Frontier Days of Old Arizona*. San Antonio, TX: Naylor Company, 1949.

Cook, James. *Fifty Years on the Old Frontier, as Cowboy, Hunter, Guide, Scout, and Ranchman*. New Haven, CT: Yale University Press, 1925.

Crisman, Harry. *Ladder of Rivers: The Story of Print Olive*. Chicago: Swallow Press, 1962.

————. *Lost Trails of the Cimarron*. Denver, CO: Swallow Press, 1961.

Crabb, Richard. *Empire on the Platte*. Cleveland, OH: World Publishing Company, 1967.

De Angelis, Gina. *The Black Cowboys*. Philadelphia, PA: Chelsea House Publishers, 1998.

Dobie, Frank. *Cow People*. Austin: University of Texas Press, 1964.

————. *The Longhorns*. Boston: Little, Brown and Company, 1941.

————. *A Vaquero of the Brush Country: Partly from the Reminiscences of John Young*. Boston: Little, Brown and Company, 1943.

Douglas, C.L. *Cattle Kings of Texas*. Dallas, TX: Cecil Baugh, 1939.

Drago, Harry. *Great American Cattle Trails*. New York: Bramhall House Publishing, 1960.

Duke, Cordia Sloan, and Joe B. Frantz. *6000 Miles of Fence: Life on the XIT Ranch of Texas*. Austin: University of Texas Press, 1961.

Durhan, Phillip, and Everett L. Jones. *The Negro Cowboys*. Lincoln: University of Nebraska Press, 1965.

Emmet, Chris. *Shanghai Pierce: A Fair Likeness*. Norman: University of Oklahoma Press, 1953.

Erwin, Allen. *The Southwest of John Horton Slaughter*. Glendale, CA: Arthur Clark Company, 1965.

Flanagan, Sue. *Trailing the Longhorns*. Austin, TX: Madrona Press, 1974.

Folsom, Franklin. *The Life and Legend of George McJunkin: Black Cowboy*. Nashville, TN: Thomas Nelson, 1973.

Ford, Davis. *The Last Cowboy: Leroy Webb*. Austin, TX: Eakin Press, 2002.

Frink, Jackson. *When Grass Was King*. Boulder: University of Colorado Press, 1957.

Gard, Wayne. *The Chisholm Trail*. Norman: University of Oklahoma Press, 1954.

Gard, Wayne, Dean Krakel, Joe Franz, Darman Winfrey, N. Frost and Don Bubar. *Along the Early Trails of the Southwest.* New York: Pemberton Press, 1969.

Glasrud, Bruce, and Michael Searles. *Black Cowboys in the American West.* Norman: University of Oklahoma Press, 2007.

Goff, Richard, and Robert McCaffree. *A Century in the Saddle.* Boulder, CO: Johnson Publishing Company 1967.

Hafen, LeRoy, and Anne Hafen. *Colorado: A Story of the State and Its People.* Denver, CO: Old West Publishing Company, 1943.

Haley, J. Evetts. *Charles Goodnight: Cowman & Plainsman.* Norman: University of Oklahoma Press, 1949.

———. *George W. Littlefield, Texan.* Norman: University of Oklahoma Press, 1943.

———. *The XIT Ranch of Texas and the Early Days of Llano Estacado.* Chicago: Lakeside Press, 1929.

Hanes, Bailey C. *Bill Pickett, Bulldogger: The Biography of a Black Cowboy.* Norman: University of Oklahoma Press, 1977.

Hendrix, John. *If I Can Do It Horseback: A Cow Country Sketchbook.* Austin: University of Texas Press, 1964.

Hough, Emerson. *The Story of the Cowboy.* New York: D. Appleton and Company, 1897.

Hunter, John Marvin, ed. *The Trail Drivers of Texas.* 2nd ed. Nashville, TN: Cokesbury Press, 1925.

Katz, William Loren. *Black People Who Made the Old West.* New York: Thomas Y. Crowell Company, 1992.

Kraisinger, Gary. *The Great Western Cattle Trail, 1874–97.* Newton, KS: Mennonite Press 2004.

Love, Nat. *The Life and Adventures of Nat Love—Better Known in the Cattle Country as "Deadwood Dick."* Lincoln: University of Nebraska Press, 1995.

Ludwig, John. *The Old Chisholm Trail.* College Station: University of Texas Press, 2018.

Maddux, Vernon. *John Hittson.* Niwot: University Press of Colorado, 1994.

Mahoney, Sylvia. *Finding the Great Western Trail.* Lubbock: Texas Tech University Press, 2015.

Massey, Sara. *Black Cowboys of Texas.* College Station: Texas A&M University Press, 2000.

McCracken, Harold. *The American Cowboy.* New York: Doubleday, 1973.

Mora, Joseph. *Trail Dust and Saddle Leather.* New York: Charles Scribner's Sons, 1946.

Myers, Walter Dean. *The Journal of Joshua Loper: A Black Cowboy*. New York: Scholastic, 1999.

Nugent, Walter. *Into the West*. New York: Knopf Publishing, 1999.

O'Neal, Bill. *Historic Ranches of the Old West*. Austin: Eakin Press, 1997.

———. *John Chisum, Frontier Cattle King*. Fort Worth: Eakin Press, 2018.

Porter, Kenneth Wiggins. *The Negro on the American Frontier*. New York: Arno Press, 1971.

Potter, Jack. *Cattle Trails of the Old West*. Edited by Laura Krehbiel. Clayton, NM: Laura Krehbiel, 1939.

Savage, W. Sherman. *Blacks in the West*. Westport, CT: Greenwood Press, 1976.

Schlissel, Lillian. *Black Frontiers: A History of African American Heroes in the Old West*. New York: Simon and Schuster, 1995.

Shelton, Richard. *Rawhider: The Story of Print Olive*. New York: Doubleday, 1992.

Siringo, Charles. *A Texas Cowboy: Fifteen Years on the Hurricane Deck of a Spanish Pony*. New York: J.S. Ogilvie Publishing Company, 1912.

Stewart, Paul, and Wallace Yvonne. *Black Cowboys*. Broomfield, CO: Phillips Publishing, 1986.

Thorp, Nathan Howard. *Pardner of the Wind*. Caldwell, ID: Caxton Printers, 1945.

Todd, Bruce. *Bones Hooks: Pioneer Negro Cowboy*. Gretna, LA: Pelican Publishing Company, 2005.

Townshend, R.B. *A Tenderfoot in Colorado*. Boulder: University Press of Colorado, 2008.

Wagner, Tricia Martineau. *Black Cowboys of the Old West*. Guilford, CT: Globe Pequot Press, 2011.

Ward, Don, ed. *Hoof Trails and Wagon Tracks*. New York: Dodd, Mead & Company, 1957.

Wukovits, John. *Legends of the West: The Black Cowboys*. New York: Chelsea House Publishing, 1997.

Wyman, Walker, and John Hart. *The Legend of Charlie Glass*. River Falls, WI: River Falls State University Press, 1970.

ABOUT THE AUTHOR

From a small Arizona ranching community, Nancy's known cowboys all her life. While there are plenty of books about cowboys and their lives, both exciting and mundane, there aren't enough about the Black cowboys. They faced the same dangers, challenges, and trouble—plus they had an additional one: the color of their skin. Bold cowboys, Black and white, joined Charles Goodnight and Oliver Loving on their daring venture, blazing a new trail and driving their longhorns to the West. Much of the Goodnight-Loving Trail in eastern New Mexico and Colorado looks as it did back in 1866. It travels through sparsely settled grasslands and rolling hills with rugged mountains in the distance. Little has changed here since thousands of longhorns passed by.

Visit us at
www.historypress.com